ACCESS

ACCESS: Accessible Course Construction for Every Student's Success is a practical guide to digital course design that incorporates and exceeds current accessibility practices for disabled and non-disabled students in higher education. Today's rapid proliferation of online, blended, and hybrid learning systems has alerted college and university staff to unforeseen yet urgent lapses in accommodating students' various learning needs and preferences. This book offers a wealth of learning design and delivery strategies that meaningfully address the notions of accessibility that move beyond compliance with the Americans With Disabilities Act (ADA). Each chapter explores accessibility in a situated context, making this an ideal resource for instructional design students and professionals, learning scientists, disability support personnel, and faculty developing their own digital courses.

Cat Mahaffey is Teaching Professor in the Writing, Rhetoric, and Digital Studies Department at the University of North Carolina at Charlotte, USA. She currently serves as President of the Global Society of Online Literacy Educators and as a Quality Matters Master Reviewer.

Ashlyn C. Walden is Senior Lecturer in the Writing, Rhetoric, and Digital Studies Department at the University of North Carolina at Charlotte, USA. She currently serves as the editor of *Research in Online Literacy Education* and is a continuing Ph.D. student in the Rhetorics, Communication, and Information Design program at Clemson University, USA.

ACCESS

Accessible Course Construction for Every Student's Success

CAT MAHAFFEY AND ASHLYN C. WALDEN

Illustrated by Ashlyn C. Walden

Routledge
Taylor & Francis Group

NEW YORK AND LONDON

Designed cover image: © Shutterstock

First published 2025
by Routledge
605 Third Avenue, New York, NY 10158

and by Routledge
4 Park Square, Milton Park, Abingdon, Oxon, OX14 4RN

Routledge is an imprint of the Taylor & Francis Group, an informa business

ISBN: 978-1-032-77935-5 (hbk)
ISBN: 978-1-032-77759-7 (pbk)
ISBN: 978-1-003-48547-6 (ebk)

DOI: 10.4324/9781003485476

Typeset in Avenir and Dante
by SPi Technologies Private Limited, India (Straive)

To our children – who have made us lifelong learners, the *why* of our work.

Contents

Authors

Cat Mahaffey is Teaching Professor in the Writing, Rhetoric and Digital Studies (WRDS) Department at the University of North Carolina at Charlotte, USA. She teaches first-year writing and courses related to privacy, information literacy, and digital design. She currently serves as President of the Global Society of Online Literacy Educators (GSOLE) and as a Quality Matters Master Reviewer (QMMR). She served on the CCCC OWI Standing Group as Associate Chair 2020–2022. In that role, she co-led a national survey on online writing instruction and collaborated with the research group to write the 2021 State of the Art of OWI Report. Her research interests include online privacy, accessibility, digital rhetoric, and technical and professional writing. Her work and research are published in *Next Steps: New Directions for/ in Writing about Writing* (2019); *Emerging Technologies in Virtual Learning Environments* (2019); and *PARS in Practice: More Resources and Strategies for Online Writing Instructors* (2020).

Ashlyn C. Walden is Senior Lecturer of the Writing, Rhetoric, and Digital Studies Department at the University of North Carolina at Charlotte. She teaches a combination of hybrid and online courses in composition, information literacy, and digital design. Beyond the classroom, Walden currently serves as editor of Research on Online Literacy Education (ROLE), a GSOLE publication. She also actively mentors faculty in digital design, course modalities, film production, and disability advocacy. Research interests primarily include digital composition and design, accessibility, critical pedagogy, disability rhetorics, and user-centered design. Her film work and research have been published in *Emerging Technologies in Virtual Learning Environments* (2019), *Journal for Multimodal Rhetorics* (2022, 2023), *Computers & Composition* (2022), and *Computers & Writing Conference Proceedings* (2023).

Introduction

Why a Course Design Book Focused on Accessibility?

We have been teaching for a while. Collectively we have nearly 25 years of experience. We share extensive course design experience, having served as administrators and faculty during the shift in education from print-based to digitally mediated classroom environments. Additionally, both of us have extensive experience developing and teaching online courses, and we've experienced online learning in our graduate studies. We live and breathe digitally mediated learning and share a strong passion for expanding educational opportunities to those that may not otherwise have access. Like all instructors, we were knocked off our axes in 2020 when the COVID-19 pandemic hit; however, we're not here to dwell on the pandemic or its aftereffects, but rather, we're here to help change the landscape of course design going forward. We hope to draw much-needed attention to designing and facilitating accessible digital course materials and course sites. Accessibility is our collective passion.

We've taught and taken courses that were less than ideal in terms of document design and course structure. We view accessibility as the grounding principle in designing any course, and in that sense, we aren't simply referring to whether or not the course meets basic ADA compliance. For us, designing an accessible course means imagining all the various students that might be in our classes, accounting for both learning preferences and needs. Our course design manual is a guidebook that seeks to bridge the gap between what we know about high-quality, effective online teaching and all other teaching modes, including face-to-face, hybrid, and hyflex. For example, we know from online teaching best practices that the work of designing an effective course is iterative, where the first design may not be effective, especially when the designer has no foundational course design experience or knowledge. However, we also know from research and experience that practice and

DOI: 10.4324/9781003485476-1

understanding of some basic design principles can go far in helping instructors become better course designers and teachers, no matter the modality, and in educating future instructional designers to design effective courses. Furthermore, we believe that approaching any course with an eye toward effective tech-mediated delivery opens up a whole new world of opportunity that is universally inclusive and accessible from the outset.

In examining the most recent course design texts, we found that not much has been written in the last two to three years that specifically addresses designing better courses. We also see the need for a book that places heavy emphasis on equity and access in regard to designing tech-mediated courses since the most recent one was Norman Coombs' (2010) book, *Designing Accessible Online Courses*. Scholars note issues of accessibility, and in particular, for a broader definition and understanding of what access is and how to perform it (Oswal & Meloncon, 2014; Hewett & DePew, 2015; Borgman & Dockter, 2018; Borgman & McArdle, 2019; Mahaffey & Walden, 2019; Walden, 2022). This book extends such scholarship by offering guidance for enacting the calls for greater accessibility, giving faculty, who are often overworked and underpaid, one resource that explains why, how, when, and where to build access in their courses.

This manual is designed as a reference guide for instructors, administrators, and instructional designers in the development of new courses and the redesign of existing courses with a focus on accessibility. We view our design manual as core text, and we envision this text as providing foundational pedagogical knowledge, tips and tricks for designing in learning management systems and utilizing other technologies, assignment guidelines, and checklists for both student accessibility and instructor/course designer reminders. Our emphasis throughout this text will be on accessible course design, and we aim to guide you, our readers, in whatever positions you hold and whatever experience level you bring in developing new courses and/or redesigning existing courses for maximum accessibility to meet the needs of students across all spectrums of ability, skill, and preparedness.

Our experience as faculty and administrators led us to the conclusion that faculty from across the disciplines may receive direct instruction and training regarding pedagogy and methods for teaching, but rarely do they receive much guidance, if any at all, into course design, particularly with attention toward digital accessibility. Furthermore, seasoned teachers understand the need for ongoing self-reflection in developing comfort and skill in the classroom, but opportunities – space and time – to do such reflection often happens haphazardly, and less-experienced teachers may not know where to start in the first place. Therefore, this manual fills these gaps by providing clear and concise approaches, based on our years of experience and in-depth research, to the kind of intricate course (re)design that many teachers want to do but don't know what to focus on or how to achieve their goals in order to make courses as accessible to students as possible.

Book Organization

In keeping with our theme of accessibility, we aimed to make the chapter structure clear and consistent. Each chapter includes the same basic subsections:

- Introduction / Overview
- What is …?
- … and Accessibility
- Methods and Application
- Model in Practice
- Putting Your Layers Together
- Checklist
- Resources and References

Introduction/Overview

Each chapter will begin with a short introduction / overview that orients the reader to the chapter topic and provides the reader with relevant context and background information.

What is …?

This section of each chapter attempts to circumvent potential course design challenges by articulating a shared understanding of the concepts discussed therein. Simply put, we aim to do more than just define key terms and concepts; instead, we unpack each design practice (e.g., scaffolding, course mapping, assignments, choosing technologies, etc.).

… and Accessibility

Since our main goal of the book is to foster a highly nuanced understanding of accessibility, we intentionally chose to include a section that situates accessibility through the lens of that chapter's theme. For example, in the

"Scaffolding" chapter, accessibility is ensuring that a diverse range of learners have a clear pathway through a course. "Content Development," on the other hand, asks how we create a course experience that is inclusive despite any potential barriers, histories, or levels of experience. We acknowledge that these two discussions of accessibility sound virtually the same, but in fact, with "Scaffolding" the accessibility focus is squarely on providing options for moving through the class, whereas "Content Development" is ensuring that all students feel included and safe.

Methods and Application

This section will be one of the more fluid sections of each chapter, with the goal of helping readers develop some concrete course content. For example, the "Navigation" chapter uses this section to first define key terms (e.g., primary, secondary, and tertiary levels of navigation) and then offer a series of heuristics to identify all levels of the course consistently and logically for all students to move through. With the "Scaffolding" chapter, we offer a framework for creating a learning sequence.

Model in Practice

To practice what we preach, we offer models in practice that readers can choose to just jump to if that is the most logical way for them to understand and apply that chapter's course design concept. In short, we offer annotated visuals that are deliberately designed to be independent of any specific composing platform or learning management system. This choice is intentional because we view accessibility as a practice beyond the constraints of any software system. Furthermore, these visuals model how to create materials that speak to different types of learners by providing readers non-textual pathways through the book.

Putting Your Layers Together

In each chapter, we do our own spin on a conclusion by stepping back and talking directly to our readers. This section will encourage them to process the chapter's theme through a lens of collaboration. Again, we are modeling the work in practice even in the construction of this book as it includes the experiences and design work of two accomplished teacher-designers. Where we are different in the competitive landscape, we see readers as collaborators, and the act of working through our book is collaboration. Readers can see how we do course design, and though they may do it differently, they are thinking through how to do their own course development.

Checklist

This section serves to further model our vision of providing multiple means of processing information. In one way, it offers a quick summary of the main points of each chapter. In another way, it allows readers to quickly determine whether the chapter in question is the right one for their needs at any point in the course design process. These checklists will help users to evaluate the impact of their design choices on students as well as provide questions for user reflection that will produce a deeper understanding of the chapter material and its application on their course design.

Resources and References

This section includes a list of references along with suggested further readings.

How to Use This Manual

This manual is not intended to be read from cover to cover. Instead, we encourage readers to review the table of contents and decide what things are important or urgent at any given time in the course (re)design process. Over time, we hope that all parts of the book will be of use to nearly every instructor or course designer, but trying to apply all our suggestions at one time may become overwhelming. Our goal is to model accessibility by meeting designers where they are, rather than leading them through processes and approaches that may not make sense for them or may frustrate them into falling back on old course designs. We offer some suggestions for using the book depending on your personal goals, as follows.

Broadening Your Definition of Accessibility: Many people define accessibility based on compliance with the American Disabilities Act (ADA). Our book will challenge you to broaden your definition of accessibility beyond just ADA compliance.

Enhance Accessibility of Existing Course Content: If your desire is to understand and/or revise your existing course materials for greater accessibility, you could focus on each chapter's accessibility section and apply the suggestions that work for you.

Redesign an Existing Assignment or Sequence: This approach is especially helpful for seasoned instructors who want to update an assignment for greater scaffolding and/or alignment of activities and assessments.

Add/Evaluate Course Technologies: If you use web tools outside your institution's domain, you'll want to look over the chapters on Online Privacy, Choosing Classroom Technologies, and Designing for Assistive Technologies.

Create a New Course: If you're starting from scratch, we recommend reviewing the chapters on Course Mapping, Scaffolding, and Content Development to give you some meaningful starting points for thinking about course design. Some folks may need to understand the whole course layout (e.g., Course Mapping), while others might want to start by designing materials (e.g., Content Development).

Increase Student Engagement: We all have classes from time to time that seem disconnected, disengaged, or perhaps confused. We recommend consulting the Engagement, Assignments, and Scaffolding chapters to address these concerns at different points in the design process.

A Few Things Before We Get Started

Before we get started with the nuts and bolts of accessibility and the many, many, many things we want to share with you about designing effective tech-mediated courses, we feel that we need to provide a brief discussion of some grounding information relevant to a book on accessible course design. We hope that you'll take a bit of time to read through this as we feel, though brief, these items are vital to helping you achieve the goals of our text as we outlined for you earlier. In the short sections that follow, we will cover:

- A definition of course design
- A brief history of distance education
- A concrete definition of accessibility as we understand and define it

What Is Course Design?

In a nutshell, course design refers to the process of creating a course, from start to finish, including

- Course materials: assignment descriptions, activities, practice lessons, lecture videos, etc.
- Course technologies: learning management systems, web tools, video and slideshow platforms, etc.
- Alignment: assignment sequences (scaffolding), grading schema, student support services, etc.
- Design: navigation (hyperlink), consistency, formatting, layout, etc.

For new instructors, some of this may sound foreign, especially since teacher preparation usually stops at the creation of a syllabus and/or course calendar, and while seasoned teachers will recognize the various aspects of course design, many of them crave guidance in one or more areas.

Distance Education History

It is important for readers to understand the inherent correspondence course nature rooted in online learning from the beginning.

From the start, distance education offered education to the masses, extending opportunities to those who may not have attended college. Technology has been the main determinant of the success of distance education as advancements in technology have allowed for more flexibility in learning outside a brick-and-mortar school, learning from a distance. Since the 2000s, there has been a growing trend in student enrollment in online education – specifically older students who are looking for more flexibility in completing their coursework (Khan & Ally, 2015; Friedman, 2016; Olson, 2016).

Defining Accessibility Historically

Lastly, as the focus of our text is accessibility, we want to leave you with a brief discussion on the definition of accessibility and our additions to the traditional way of defining accessibility. The Americans With Disabilities

Act (ADA) was signed into law by President George H. W. Bush in 1990 and updated in 2010 to include ADA Standards for Accessible Design. ADA provides people with mental or physical (dis)abilities the "same opportunities as everyone else to participate in the mainstream of American life," including employment and access to public services, commercial facilities, and transportation (ADA National Network, 2021). The act was intended to provide individuals with (dis)abilities the same rights as those enjoyed by others and is similar to Title VII of the Civil Rights Act of 1964 (ADA National Network, 2021). We believe this definition of accessibility is too narrow and confining, and despite its good intentions, ultimately supports a view of the world that is inherently ableist. Such approaches unfortunately give way to checklist behaviors that treat accessibility as an afterthought and not a grounding design and pedagogical principle. It also fails to recognize that many challenges in learning aren't necessarily neatly defined and visible, yet their impacts are nonetheless tangible.

Redefining Accessibility

Accessibility as a term often gets lumped into a focus on ADA compliance, as discussed earlier, and accommodating students with physical or cognitive (dis)abilities. However, to us, accessibility is so much more than ADA compliance. Accessibility spans many areas of designing, instructing, and/or administering tech-mediated courses. Historically a lot of the responsibility of accessing content was placed on the student, but we feel it's important to shift at least part of the responsibility from students to instructors for errors and failures involving course navigation, assignments, and submissions. In short, finding content in the course should not be a barrier to learning.

Thus, we as the authors of this text hold a more expanded definition of accessibility:

> Accessibility refers to the ease of entry and use of a product, service, space, or text; and considers course design (navigation, layout, color scheme, font type, font emphasis), course tools (applications, discussion forums, quizzes) and course materials (instructional texts, resources, assignment descriptions, submission and evaluation guidelines). Thus, an accessible tech-mediated course is one that affords every learner the opportunity to succeed, regardless of technological skill, reading level, native language, learning preference, or physical impairment.
>
> (Mahaffey & Walden, 2019)

Yet, simply discussing how we wish to expand the definition of accessibility may not be useful, so it is necessary to articulate several concrete practices that any course designer may use in their tech-mediated classes no matter what the subject area:

- Redundancy is key – providing students with multiple reminders in different places of the course improves access
- Re-examine how course texts are provided to students to ensure that students can use screen readers and interact with the texts in ways they prefer (i.e., reading online or reading in print)
- When creating documents, use the styles feature so that there are headings, titles, subtitles, etc.
- Model and practice user-centered design in digital spaces to create a course that can be easily navigated
- Have a conversation with students about accessibility and complicate students' perceptions of what accessibility means in the context of your course – that it extends to users' learning preferences and needs too (not just physical/cognitive (dis)abilities)
- Re-examine the use of color in the online course materials (allow for adequate color contrast to accommodate for those with visual impairments and/or color-blindness)
- Examine access routes, that is, how many clicks it takes to get to the important content in a course.

Models in Practice

A core tenet of our course design approaches is founded on developing a course and materials that model for students the concepts and skills we wish them to practice. In this spirit, we conclude this introduction by offering a model for navigating this book, given our strengths, weaknesses, and interests (Figures 0.1 and 0.2).

Despite the differences in our course design and development preferences, one aspect that we thrive on as teacher-designers is collaboration. You will see throughout this book we encourage levels of collaboration, whether it's colleague to colleague, teacher to student, students to teachers, in large groups, or with partners. Cat and Ashlyn have done some degree of all of these and have found them immensely powerful in understanding and enacting accessibility. That said, we realize that collaboration is not always possible for various reasons. But we hope this book offers you a point of asynchronous

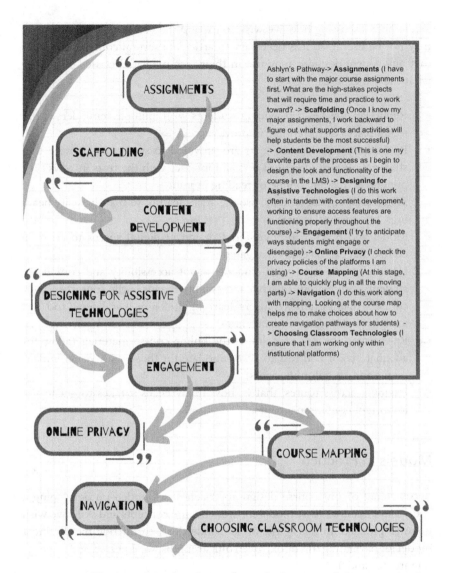

Figure 0.1 Ashlyn's preferred pathway through the manual. You can see that she starts thinking about things like navigation and assignments early in her process, while navigation and choosing classroom technologies come later

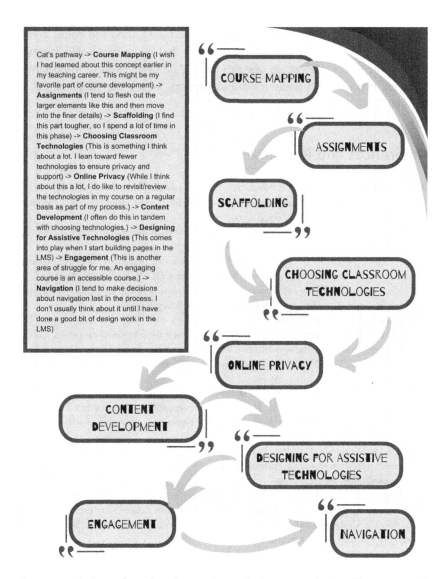

Cat's pathway -> **Course Mapping** (I wish I had learned about this concept earlier in my teaching career. This might be my favorite part of course development) -> **Assignments** (I tend to flesh out the larger elements like this and then move into the finer details) -> **Scaffolding** (I find this part tougher, so I spend a lot of time in this phase) -> **Choosing Classroom Technologies** (This is something I think about a lot. I lean toward fewer technologies to ensure privacy and support) -> **Online Privacy** (While I think about this a lot, I do like to revisit/review the technologies in my course on a regular basis as part of my process.) -> **Content Development** (I often do this in tandem with choosing technologies.) -> **Designing for Assistive Technologies** (This comes into play when I start building pages in the LMS) -> **Engagement** (This is another area of struggle for me. An engaging course is an accessible course.) -> **Navigation** (I tend to make decisions about navigation last in the process. I don't usually think about it until I have done a good bit of design work in the LMS)

COURSE MAPPING

ASSIGNMENTS

SCAFFOLDING

CHOOSING CLASSROOM TECHNOLOGIES

ONLINE PRIVACY

CONTENT DEVELOPMENT

DESIGNING FOR ASSISTIVE TECHNOLOGIES

ENGAGEMENT

NAVIGATION

Figure 0.2 Cat's preferred pathway through the manual. She likes to spend time mapping out the course and, like Ashlyn, works on assignments as some of the first stages of her course design process. She considers engagement and navigation as later stages

collaboration with us as scholars, teachers, and designers. You come to this book with different experiences and expertise that we cannot possibly anticipate. Trust your instincts. Be open to ideas. And perhaps most importantly, look for ways to find connection and support, which are fundamental to accessibility.

References and Resources

ADA National Network. (2021, Nov.). *What is the American with Disabilities Act (ADA).* Information, guidance, and training on the American with Disabilities Act. https://adata.org/learn-about-ada

Borgman, J., & Dockter, J. (2018). Considerations of access and design in the online writing classroom. *Computers and Composition, 2018*(4), 94–105.

Borgman, J., & McArdle, C. (Eds.). (2019). *Personal, accessible, responsive, strategic: Resources and strategies for online writing instructors.* Fort Collins, CO: WAC Clearinghouse.

Coombs, N. (2010). *Making online teaching accessible: Inclusive course design for students with disabilities* (pp. 178–181). San Francisco, CA: John Wiley & Sons.

Friedman, J. (Ed.). (2016, January). U.S. news releases 2016 best online programs. *U.S. News and World Report.* Retrieved from https://www.usnews.com/education/online-education/articles/us-news-ranks-best-online-programs

Hewett, B., & DePew, K. (2015). *Foundational practices in online writing instruction.* WAC Clearinghouse.

Khan, B., & Ally, M. (2015). *The handbook of e-learning* (Vol. 1). New York, NY: Routledge.

Mahaffey, C., & Walden, A. (2019). # teachingbydesign: Complicating accessibility in the tech-mediated classroom. In K. Becnel (Ed.), *Emerging technologies in virtual learning environments* (pp. 38–66). Hershey, PA: IGI Global.

Oswal, S., & Meloncon, L. (2014). Paying attention to accessibility when designing online courses in technical and professional communication. *Journal of Business and Technical Communication, 28*(3), 271–300.

Olson, S. A. (2016, May). Higher learning across three generations. *Sky Magazine,* 129–137.

Walden, A. C. (2022). Necessity is the mother of invention: Accessibility pre, inter, & post pandemic. *Computers and Composition, 66,* 102740. Accessed January 30, 2024. https://doi.org/10.1016/j.compcom.2022.102740

Content Development　　1

Introduction/Overview

This chapter offers multiple strategies for developing content for your course. As in the other areas we discuss in this book, this part of course design is more relevant to some instructors than others, and more relevant to some courses you teach than others. For your courses designed around textbooks or programs that provide content, this chapter will help you evaluate how/if the textbook/software actually fulfills the purposes of the course, supports you as the instructor, and addresses accessibility issues for students. For courses that you have carte blanche to develop from the ground up, this chapter is crucial in terms of helping you manage your workload and helping you make judicious decisions about what to adopt, adapt, or create. The key here is to not see the opportunity to develop an entire course as a painful exercise in which you build everything yourself. You must be open to prioritizing, knowing that with every iteration of the course you might choose to develop certain parts from scratch and not others. Finally, for courses that have some standardization such as core assignments or specific learning outcomes, we will again emphasize strategies for how to best use your time in the creation, augmentation, or wholesale adoption of course content and materials specifically with regards to your personal strengths as an instructor.

Our aim here is to help instructors select texts and resources for a course, including when/if students should buy a textbook/software and whether instructors should use open access sources. We will also emphasize accessibility as, partly, a sustainable practice of collecting resources that don't always require the instructor to develop materials solely on their own. Now, we have to be transparent here as writers of this book: the desire to create all of her own content is a real struggle for Ashlyn. This comes from a place of wanting to provide maximum accessibility for her students, but such labor caused by

DOI: 10.4324/9781003485476-2

one small adjustment to the design and/or content can lead to a cascade effect of changes that are not sustainable for any instructor. Cat, on the other hand, is always seeking opportunities to collaborate with others and import materials/resources from other reputable sources. Both methods are valid, while also presenting a unique series of challenges that we will explore throughout this chapter. In any case, accessibility being the key grounding principle is important, but this cannot come at the expense of making smart working decisions about what to develop versus curate/adapt for now versus later.

What Is Content Development?

For our purposes, content development refers to the work of curating, adapting, and/or creating lessons, activities, assignments, and resources for your course. Again, the level at which you adopt, adapt, or create is contingent upon your comfort level/expertise with the subject matter and course design, restrictions placed on the course at the department or institutional level, and your own personal preferences as a teacher-designer. With this in mind, it might help if you begin with the strategies we lay out in our "Course Mapping" chapter first, plotting any non-negotiable requirements such as assignments or course learning objectives. Doing so will help you get a larger sense of what the course looks like as a whole so you can see spaces where extra scaffolding is needed, how close due dates should be assigned, and the type of feedback and grades turnaround most appropriate for your course. Considering these factors first is imperative in part because it will help you decide where you want to spend your time (e.g., locating ready-made open-source resources, creating your own, or relying on a text that must be purchased by students). In the case where you are provided a fairly rigid course shell and structure, starting with the "Course Mapping" chapter might still help simply because it can reveal just how much room you actually have to insert your own course content elements. This is where supplemental texts and nontraditional resources such as videos or interactive games might be appropriate.

Course content development cannot be completed in isolation from the overall structure of the class because it limits the ability to effectively create a cohesive learning experience (Wiggins & McTighe, 2005; Ambrose et al., 2010; Fink, 2013; Reid & Maybee, 2022). You may find working through this chapter will require you to flip back and forth between "Course Mapping" and "Scaffolding" because both will help you see where and how to best devote your content development time. For example, your course map would be a great place to mark your ideal preferences for adopting, adapting, or creating materials/assignments for your class. From here, as you decide based on your own knowledge of the class or in collaboration with more experienced colleagues, note where the most scaffolding is needed, then readjust your notes on adopt/adapt/create. Finally, when you sit down to actually develop the content, make adjustments to your notations as needed in terms of your own time and comfort level. Sometimes it's okay to leave something for creation for another cycle of teaching the course. For example, let's say you are teaching a research methods course in history. Students in the class would need to know how to conduct documentary, archival, oral history, and biographical research, which are common methods across the social sciences. In this case, an adoption of a research methodology text in history would be appropriate as would another text that discusses methods of social science research more generally. Adaptations to a more general text could be supplemented by additional resources created by the instructor or located online and open access. Where a teacher might spend some time creating materials would be from their own research interests modeling how they would (or have) conducted research that meets these differing methods.

We acknowledge – like many of the other chapters in this text – content development is time-consuming and challenging. It is, also and perhaps more importantly, worthwhile and rewarding. Thoughtfully curated, modified, or developed course content is integral to any class not only for students but for you as the instructor who can steadily build a repertoire of materials that can be substituted out or revised on the fly as needed.

Content Development and Accessibility

Your decisions about what type of content to include or create can have ripple effects with regard to accessibility. First and foremost, students struggle to grasp course content they cannot connect to their own experiences and perspectives (Freeman et al., 2007; Johnson et al., 2007; Strayhorn, 2012; Reid & Maybee, 2022; Yu, 2022). Consider a first-year seminar course that is made up of mostly traditional, college-age students 18–22, and one adult returning veteran using their GI Bill to further their education. Even amongst the 18–22-year-olds in the class, experience can vary widely. Some may be fresh out of high school, others from home school, some commuters, others residential, and all may come from vastly different socioeconomic, cultural, and racial backgrounds as well. In short, the senior repeating the course for the second time in hopes of graduating will likely view the class very differently than the 18-year-old fresh out of high school. Add to that a student who has just come out of active-duty military in a combat zone, and the multiplicity of opportunities to include or exclude students becomes a complex reality. By no means is it possible to account for every potential configuration of student experience, but what this example shows is that we need to be careful, no matter the subject area, when choosing materials that only target the stereotypical college freshman.

There is another aspect of learning when considering accessibility as well, and that is classroom climate. The type of content you expose students to can nurture interaction and encourage community, or make some students feel marginalized or insulted (Ambrose et al., 2010; Hurtado et al., 2012; Booker, 2016; Thomas, 2018). For example, say you are teaching a planning and curriculum course for special education in K-12 public schools; this course will likely encompass planning for a diverse group of students that have a range of physical, intellectual, and cognitive disabilities, as well as potentially high-performing gifted students. Focusing largely on curricular planning in regard to physical disabilities (e.g., visible) within the class could make some students feel marginalized because their disability isn't visible. The problematic nature of this example goes a step further: it fosters an ableist insensitivity that can then be perpetuated by learners outside of the classroom. Think *Rain Man*. Obviously all people with autism have savant-like qualities, so when Ashlyn's son doesn't demonstrate similar characteristics, something is defective in him as a person. By no means do we as teacher-designers ascribe to this line of thinking, but the abhorrent nature of the example still holds: it is essential to consider texts and support resources that present diverse perspectives, voices, and experiences because it fosters inclusivity and cultural sensitivity. Furthermore, we assert that accessibility as an intentional part of course design and instruction is essential no matter what the subject area is. An engineering class must provide materials that are accessible to a wide range of student needs and preferences; that student with low vision, for example, must be able to use a screen reader to engage with course material, which may require some adjustment on the part of the instructor-designer. Beyond making the material inclusive in such a way that it limits (or eliminates) marginalization, the engineering faculty member must be transparent about these choices with students because such design for inclusivity it serves as a model for the novice engineer. Accessibility in content development thus becomes an integral practice of solid course design and a model for how students can create inclusive texts (lab reports, memos, graphic reports, flyers, financial analyses, proposals, or some other genre we've yet to invent) beyond the classroom.

Perhaps the most important concern regarding content and accessibility relates to economics. Students who cannot afford to purchase an expensive textbook or software face barriers of access that cannot be understated. They may resort to borrowing from classmates or using a library copy of the book or a library computer, all of which require additional labor and time for such students. While most institutions have public computer labs or loan programs for laptops and accompanying software, space or access are not always guaranteed. Coupled with the fact that most of these machines require backup of saving processes external to the device itself, the time and labor quickly mounts. Then of course there is the issue of mobile devices sometimes being the primary medium from which a student works on your class. Tablets, like smartphones, are considered a part of this category as they do not have the same memory or processing power of a standard computer. App versions of required programs may be available, but their aspect ratio, nesting of essential information architecture (e.g., file, save, edit, word count, etc.), and functionality can vary widely. Even certain user features such as notifications or dark modes can wreak havoc on the accessibility of course content. When we discuss inequities in higher education, this particular barrier may be one of the most avoidable. This is not to say that adopting a textbook or software is always the wrong choice, but it must be a thoroughly vetted choice. Our goal here is to offer guidance in making these choices so that you can balance your content needs alongside the needs of your students, and cost should be among one of the chief access concerns. Assuming that students who are in college have access to campus resources, and perhaps have financial aid, is not an invitation to choose material that may otherwise be cost prohibitive.

Finally, in this area of course design, concerns around accessibility include your own labor and sustainable work/life balance. One benefit of using ready-to-go open access content is that students can learn to draw upon those resources as they continue to grow as scholars and professionals. Too often the heavy lifting of creating content falls onto the backs of contingent faculty who are already overworked and underpaid. In this way, the notion of accessible content means much more than students being able to locate and use it; it also means that instructors' expertise as subject matter experts toward feedback and assessment aren't overwhelmed by the labor of creating content. Again, balance is key. Yes, it may be that you are best positioned to make a resource on the finer points of universal design in a human-centered design class in computing and informatics. But the fact that you also have a teaching load of four classes all with different preps along with other professional projects or personal life goals you are working on may necessitate the use of ready-made open access materials. However, seeking out these materials (or adapting them) does still require the attention to access we mentioned earlier: multiple perspectives must be included that are attentive to issues of race, class, age, gender, technological skill sets, and (dis)ability. Any good teacher knows that the most successful classes are the ones that invite students in, rather than stamping their issues of difference and expression out.

Methods and Application

We come to content development along a continuum. On one end, we might be handed a course that includes content previously developed and taught. On the other end, we might be asked to develop a new course and start from nothing. Somewhere in the middle, you might be given a set of non-negotiable assignments or objectives that have to be included, but how you teach to or scaffold toward these activities is up to the instructor. No matter where you find yourself on this continuum, we recommend that you put some attention toward how much content to adopt, how much content to adapt, and how much content you should create from scratch. This again, is a space where we would encourage you to review the strategies in the "Course Mapping" chapter and mark items for each of these three areas. It can help you get a sense of the volume of work/planning that's needed, and then you can make adjustments from there given the timeline you are working toward for your class.

For clarity, *adopting content* refers to the act of using ready-to-go assignments and resources, which can be in the form of a textbook, supplemental materials like videos or handouts, or even an assignment. For example, Cat regularly collaborates with her colleague, Gretchen, on assignments and even feedback strategies; both use the same guidelines and assessment loops that provide a rich comparative analysis on what worked/didn't work such that the labor of making adjustments is significantly less.

Adapting content happens when an instructor edits, adds to, or removes parts of existing resources to more appropriately meet learning outcomes or support a particular student population. Ashlyn has learned to live more comfortably in this space rather than creating whole worlds of immersion based on original content building. Though she does some similar assignments as Cat (and by extension, Gretchen), she often makes tweaks to the assignment to fit with some of her overarching goals. For Cat and Gretchen, slowing down the inquiry research process is key, so more time is spent summarizing and reflecting on source material, whereas Ashlyn truncates the research process and focuses more on synthesizing research to examine where gaps exist. Both are appropriate given the strengths and goals each instructor has.

Creating content is the most labor-intensive approach where you find yourself writing new lessons and resources based on your own subject matter expertise. While this can be incredibly rewarding – simply because we all have spent way too many hours trying to locate just the right resource that doesn't yet exist – it can be a massive energy drain. Ashlyn can speak to this cycle all too well; in short, it is not necessary to create a highly immersive learning experience that is so granular to the specific course experience that application outside of the class becomes a problem. Consider the fact that discussing the principles of universal design through the lens of developing a writing portfolio becomes problematic because it doesn't take the leap of generalizing the knowledge to the point of a student knowing that alt text is needed for an artifact pictured in their archeology paper.

In this section, we will discuss strategies for determining when/how to adopt, adapt, or create new content. We want to emphasize that this process may shift depending on what iteration of the course you are dealing with – is it a first-round teaching experience or old hat and round 30? Perhaps it's somewhere in the middle, where you feel comfortable with the content of the class, but your design skills are still lacking. We invite you to come to this process taking into account your own skill level with design and subject matter, as well as the specific needs and preferences of the populations you are teaching.

Content Criteria: When to Do What

Let's address the elephant in the room. Textbooks and software can be expensive. The textbook and software industries are fraught with issues. Concerns about student debt are valid. For this reason, when you can, we encourage you to choose open access resources rather than adopting expensive materials or platforms.

Having said that, sometimes it's necessary and appropriate to have students purchase a textbook or program for your course. There are many factors that go into this decision. First, consider your own workload. Adapting or creating new content requires labor and time that you may or may not have, depending on your teaching load and number of course preps. If you've found yourself struggling to make a decision, we encourage you to give yourself permission to protect your own mental health and well-being by adopting a textbook if one is available, regardless of its cost. This is especially important for the first time you teach a given course when the assignments and goals are less clear. That said, once you locate a text or platform you want to use, we encourage you to reach out to them to see what options they may offer for bulk purchase, see if they are available from third-party vendors at a lesser price, and then share this information on your course materials list. Later, when you have time, and have taught the course at least once and receive feedback from students, we encourage you to overlay this chapter onto the textbook or software program to see whether it's really meeting the needs of your students, your needs as the instructor of record, and the course objectives and outcomes.

Whether you choose a textbook, program, or open access resources, you'll want to evaluate it according to the following criteria:

• Ensure that it offers proper representation across race, gender, ability, age, class, and culture. Review the reading and reference lists to ensure that diverse voices and perspectives are included. Issues of ability, age, and gender can sometimes be scant in certain subject areas, so when you find material that relates to the other areas, we encourage you to then supplement to address the missing criteria.

• Consider whether/how the lessons and resources match the learning needs of your student population. In short, who is your student population, and has their makeup changed? Think about how much student needs and preferences have changed post-pandemic. In this case, as well as others, open access resources might work for lower-level, introductory courses, while at the same time being too basic for upper-level courses.

• Weigh the cost of a textbook against how much of it students will actively use/need. One of the biggest complaints from students is that they are required to purchase textbooks and then only use a small percentage of the content. Our recommendation is that the text or program should be used up to 75% of its total capacity. Less than that, it becomes an issue, no matter if the cost is relatively low. Think of it this way: in some classes, students have required materials that can be upwards of hundreds of dollars, thus savings in one area can ultimately help in another. No, it isn't always our responsibility to think about what other teachers are assigning, but just imagine if we all took this approach how much more beneficial this would be for students.

If you find issues or shortcomings with any of the preceding criteria, it's time to consider adapting the content for more appropriateness or creating new content altogether. The first bullet, for example, notes how issues of ability, gender, and age are sometimes absent in source material, and we made the suggestion of adding additional, ready-made supplementary material. But what if solid supplemental material doesn't exist, or isn't developed to the extent that is needed for your course? Think for a moment about a curated digital portfolio for a writing class. Yes, the focus of the portfolio is to showcase student work progression and use reflective writing to draw connections about growth and composing processes, but an accessibility approach also demands work with the visual design. Alt text, images, leveled headings, white space, color contrast (all of which are explored more in the "Assignments" chapter), are needed to produce a text that is rhetorically aware of audience needs and preferences. One might use a series of graphic design videos to teach about organization, color contrast, and the use of images, but as the instructor, you might also provide additional context as to what color contrast means in a written document, how organization can be developed using shapes to house related materials, and why images are important for communicating meaning to the more highly visual audience member, while at the same time including alt text to not exclude those with visual challenges.

Adapting content can quickly become just as time consuming as creating content, especially when you find yourself changing more than a quarter of what the original resource offers. Use the following criteria to help you evaluate both the feasibility and effectiveness of content adaptation:

- Note gaps in the representation of voices represented. Are there particular voices that are glaringly absent? If the initial answer is no, this might be a good time to invite a colleague to assess with you. The chances are, no matter how careful, someone – intentionally or not – is left out. For Ashlyn, when (dis)ability is missing from core content, she often adapts material to include this element because it is within her wheelhouse of expertise.
- Articulate your wheelhouses of expertise. A good determiner of whether or not adaptation or adoption is needed relies heavily on your own experience and knowledge of the subject area. AI–assisted writing, for example, is an emerging area of study for many professionals, thus an adaptive approach might be more difficult. This is where we would then encourage you to go back to the adoption route.
- Weigh the amount of work needed for adaptation. Does the text/resource/platform need more than a 25% overhaul of some sort? Do you see yourself supplementing more than 75% of the material? If the answer is yes to either one of these questions, do not collect $200, do not go past go – return to the adoption route. If the adoption route is still unfruitful, then it may be time to create some content. However, if what you are looking at requires minor supplementation of 25% or less, we recommend adapting the material to your needs. Adapting existing materials is also a great way to hone your chops in preparation for ground-up content development, while operating at an implicit collaborative level.

Say you have now hit the point where adoption or adaptation is not feasible. The material you have consulted is subpar at best, flat nonexistent, or is perhaps fraught with issues of understandability to your student population (this is where choosing a discipline-specific academic article may do more harm than good). Let's say that in addition to not being able to adopt or adapt you also found that you have extra time in your schedule (we know – you are teachers like us, and you are probably laughing out loud). But the truth is, sometimes we push ourselves to make time for the parts of course preparation that really mean something to us as instructors. So whether that time exists either in theory or fact, we invite you to carve out a space for attempting to create content for your courses at least once a year. This content creation does not have to be some sort of earth-shattering endeavor; it can be a quick cheat sheet, a graphic, a screencast of assignment guidelines, the creation of a course FAQs forum – the possibilities are endless.

As we noted previously, creating content is the most labor-intensive approach to course design, but it can also be one of the most rewarding in that it forces you to become the student once more. In other words, "How can I best describe the chemical reaction of an acid and base in this chemistry class without using a tactile demonstration?" That's where the following questions become more helpful in determining the appropriateness of creating content versus adapting or adopting.

- What gaps exist in the core content that do not address different learning needs and preferences? Think in terms of learning styles: visual, aural, spatial, tactile, or collaborative. Now, addressing each one of these potential learning needs is daunting no doubt, but we encourage you to start with just one at a time, and slowly build toward completion for differing learners the more you teach the course. Using the chemistry example, the auditory-preferred student may benefit from a voice recording that describes the process to go along with a visual created in the form of an infographic.
- Does your specific area of expertise have a perspective that is absent from the content you have curated or adapted? If the answer is yes, this may be a great time to develop a small-scale resource / activity / assignment to bridge the missing content.
- Weigh the time needed for the desired content creation against your own workload and goals for the course and prioritize. Is it necessary to have an infographic of sorts or a slides presentation with every major assignment – maybe not. But, taking time to create a resource for the one assignment that tends to give students the most trouble is time well spent (Figures 1.1–1.3).

Model in Practice (Figures 1.1–1.3)

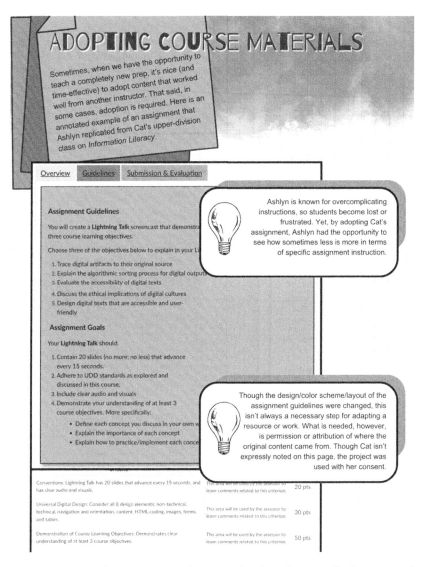

Figure 1.1 A sample assignment that was developed originally by Cat and then adopted by Ashlyn. The only changes to the assignment were with the color scheme and basic design

ADAPTING COURSE MATERIALS

Adapting course content comes in handy when you don't want to "reinvent the wheel," but perhaps you have found a particular style of wheel that works well for you. In fact, adapting materials is commonplace for most teacher-designers. Here is a sample assignment that Cat adapted for a First-Year Writing course.

Cat and Ashlyn have often collaborated on course materials with one another and others. This particular assignment started out as a practice assignment to help student familiarize themselves with the library.

The original version developed by colleagues Gretchen Pratt and Linda Hoffman gave a basic introduction to the resources available. Over time, Cat has expanded this assignment extensively over time.

When first adapting materials, ask yourself how you might simplify, streamline, or emphasize certain information? Consider how the item might given you insight into other similar aspects of your course to help you develop some specific templates, rubrics, or expectations.

For Cat, revising this assignment over time also revealed opportunities to create a type of activity for students that requires extensive note-taking.

Step 1

Explore the Digital Resources of the Library

1. Go to the Atkins Library homepage and click on the box at the top with three lines.
2. Explore the resources by expanding each section and learning about how to do the following. **Be sure to take notes for your reflection:**
   1. How to reserve a study room
   2. How to checkout a book
   3. How to request items
   4. How to borrow a laptop
   5. What Area 49 includes
   6. How to get help with research
   7. How to print copies in the library

You should have **notes** from Step 1.

Step 2

Go on a **scavenger hunt** by spending at least **one hour in the physical library**. During that time, please do the following:

1. Go up to the 10th floor, and **take a photo** of the Charlotte skyline.
2. Search for and check out a book from the shelf (this can be a book for your Inquiry Research Project, for another class, or just a book you'd like to read on your own.) If you have trouble locating the book, be sure to ask a librarian for help. **Take a photo** of the book you check out.
3. Visit the ground floor, and **take notes** on how the workspaces are being used.
4. Visit the main floor and the 2nd floor, **taking notes** on how students use these spaces.
5. Find your favorite place in the library, and spend some time working there. **Take a photo/selfie** of the place you've chosen.

You should have **5 artifacts** in the form of photos, selfies and notes from Step 2.

Step 3

Process what you have learned.

Write a reflection of about 300 words responding to the questions below.

- Look back over the notes you took in Step 1. What did you find helpful?
- What was your impression of Atkins Library before you visited? Did your impression change after your time there? Did anything surprise you? Frustrate you?
- What did you notice about how students use the library?
- What role might the library play in creating a sense of community on campus?
- What was your favorite place in the library and why? What did you do while you were there?
- How and why might you use the library in the future?

Figure 1.2 Library resources activity developed by two of Cat and Ashlyn's colleagues, Gretchen Pratt and Linda Hofmann. Changes to the assignment have been made over time to make it increasingly useful to students as well as impacting how other similar assignments were adapted

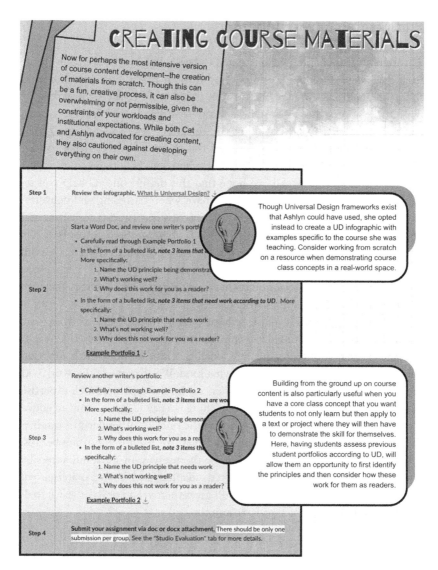

Figure 1.3 An assignment developed from scratch by Ashlyn. For some courses, students struggle to connect concepts to practice, and as such, developing original materials helps make explicit connections to other coursework

Putting Your Layers Together

Throughout this chapter, we have tried to be deliberate about what it means to adopt, adapt, and create content and how to make judicious choices of these three options. Granted, it is possible that your freedom to move through these three approaches to content development may be restricted to varying degrees, but the truth is that there is often much more wiggle room than we sometimes imagine. The purpose of this chapter is not to make you feel inadequate or overly restricted no matter where you fall on the course development continuum. Instead, we hope that this discussion will help you see just how much agency you actually do have when designing and delivering your content. We also want to once again stress the importance of mental, emotional, and intellectual labor expended when we prepare courses. Too often, instructors are asked to do more for less all under the guise of serving the rapidly changing needs of our students. And while laudable, it can create an oppressive loop of responsibility that is neither supported or recognized by the institution and sometimes students.

That said, doing this level of content development is still worth it – it's just a question of how much, what kind, and when. Sometimes it's okay to take those three questions separately, dealing with the "how much adoption, adaptation, and creation" instead of what kind. We all come to this work with differing learning and teaching experiences, levels of subject area expertise, and with personal lives all our own. Teaching is a privilege, as many an educator would extol, but it should not come at the price of other parts of our lives that make life worth living. Such a model in and of itself is important because it helps students set boundaries even for themselves. In short, an accessible course design with a mixture of adopted, adapted, and created materials will make for a learning experience that still gives them – and us – the space to do what they love outside of the classroom too.

Checklist

- [ ] Choose readings and resources that represent students with diverse backgrounds, abilities, and learning needs.
- [ ] When possible, consider materials that are affordable or provide alternatives to expensive textbooks, such as open educational resources, library resources, or your own created content.
- [ ] Consider resources that can be reused or adapted for future iterations of the course. Look for materials that allow for customization, remixing, and updating to meet changing needs.

Readings and Resources

Ambrose, S. A., Bridges, M. W., DiPietro, M., Lovett, M. C., & Norman, M. K. (2010). *How learning works: Seven research-based principles for smart teaching.* San Francisco, CA: Jossey-Bass.

Booker, K. (2016). Connection and commitment: How sense of belonging and classroom community influence degree persistence for African American undergraduate women. *International Journal of Teaching and Learning in Higher Education, 28*(2), 218–299. http://www.isetl.org/ijtlhe/

Fink, L. D. (2013). *Creating significant learning experiences: An integrated approach to designing college courses.* San Francisco, CA: Jossey-Bass.

Freeman, T. M., Anderman, L. H., & Jensen, J. M. (2007). Sense of belonging in college freshmen at the classroom and campus levels. *Journal of Experimental Education, 75*(3), 203–220.

Hurtado, S., Alvarez, C. L., Guillermo-Wann, C., Cuellar, M., & Arellano, L. (2012). A model for diverse learning environments. In *Higher education: Handbook of theory and research* (Vol. 27, pp. 41–122). Dordrecht: Springer.

Johnson, D. R., Soldner, M., Leonard, J. B., Alvarez, P., Inkelas, K. K., Rowan-Kenyon, H. T., & Longerbeam, S. D. (2007). Examining sense of belonging among first-year undergraduates from different racial/ethnic groups. *Journal of College Student Development, 48*(5), 525–542.

Reid, P. & Maybee, C. (2022). Textbooks and course materials: A holistic 5-step selection process, *College Teaching, 70*(4), 518–529, https://doi.org/10.1080/87567555.2021.1987182

Strayhorn, T. L. (2012). *College students' sense of belonging: A key to educational success for all students.* New York, NY: Routledge.

Thomas, K. C. (2018). *Rethinking student belonging in higher education: From Bourdieu to Borderlands* (1st ed.). New York, NY: Routledge.

Wiggins, G. P., & McTighe, J. (2005). *Understanding by design* (2nd ed.). Alexandria, VA: Association for Supervision and Curriculum Development.

Wiley, D., & Hilton III, J. L. (2018). Defining OER-enabled pedagogy. *International Review of Research in Open and Distance Learning, 19*(4), 133–147. https://doi.org/10.19173/irrodl.v19i4.3601

Yu, E. (2022). The impact of culturally inclusive pedagogy on student achievement in a multicultural urban school setting. *Urban Education (Beverly Hills, Calif.), 57*(1), 135–153. https://doi.org/10.1177/0042085918804013

Assignments   **2**

Introduction/Overview

This chapter offers strategies for presenting assignments to students, including writing assignment descriptions from a student's perspective, creating multiple pathways for processing and understanding expectations, and clarifying those expectations so students can move toward assessment. Depending on how you're moving through this book, you may find yourself working on assignment creation at different points in your process. For example, Cat often begins with course mapping, then works backwards to flesh out assignments. Ashlyn, on the other hand, prefers to outline the particulars of every major assignment, develop resources, and build the assignment look in the learning management system (LMS), then work toward mapping the course. We find this chapter to be complementary to both the Scaffolding and Content Development chapters, so you may find it helpful to look at these three chapters together, moving back and forth between them as it makes sense for your own course goals and design practices.

When we think about assignments, we approach this work from a multi-layered perspective. Our discussions of assignments includes capstone work that aligns with learning outcomes, mid-level assignments that might require feedback and revision, and small-scale tasks that introduce a skill/concept, then allow some low-stakes practice. Beyond the types of assignments, this chapter asks you to think about assignments in terms of instructional guidelines, resources/models, evaluation criteria, and the physical layout of the activity or task. When viewed holistically, these layers create an increasingly complex development task for us as instructors, while at the same time providing redundancies and support for students in a way that helps them be successful. Like many of the other areas we cover in this book, it's easy to

DOI: 10.4324/9781003485476-3

become overwhelmed by the sheer volume of work that goes into effective assignment development.

Fret not. Part of the reason we are able to speak to this level of specificity is that we have two brains and many years of experience and expertise in different areas of course development. Combined together, it's much easier for us to project the layers necessary for a well-developed series of assignments – hence why we again encourage you to collaborate with colleagues. The two of us have varying strengths in the area of assignment development, things like creating resources that are accessible; writing assignment descriptions that are comprehensive, concise, and clear; and designing the layout and presentation of assignment guidelines. That said, you may not be an in a situation where you can devote time to collaborating with others on this level where one might be responsible for design, another for concision, and so on, and if that is the case, we encourage you to consider what makes up a successful assignment first, then work toward the other layers as time and practice allow. Note that this process may unfold over many semesters or cycles as you teach your courses, and this is a perfectly reasonable way to approach assignment design in a way that is sustainable.

What Makes Up a Successful Assignment?

In a nutshell, the efficacy of an assignment is determined by student success (Kuh et al., 2006; York et al., 2015; Muniz et al., 2017; MacNaul et al., 2021). Period. Factors that impact student success include a combination of what *they* bring to an assignment – previous knowledge, practice, critical thinking skill, and so on (Muniz et al., 2017; Al-Abyadh & Azeem, 2022) – and how *you* present, explain, and/or support them through its stages (Kuh et al., 2006; York et al., 2015). You can only control the latter part of the equation in how you write/design your assignments, but you should also strive to understand that students come to you with a wide range of experiences and skill sets. Too often, we've seen teachers blame students when their assignments fail, when in reality, reasons for shortfalls in the classroom are complex. We say all this to point you toward the notion of student-centered assignment design (Middleton & Reiff, 1985; Hewett, 2015; TILT Higher Ed Examples and Resources, 2015). When we step back and put ourselves into the shoes of our students, we gain clarity as to not only *what* to include in an assignment description but also *how* to explain our goals and the steps necessary for successful completion of the assignment.

A successful assignment is one that clearly explains **why** the assignment is being given, **where** that assignment fits into the course's learning goals, and **how** to successfully complete the assignment. And that last one, the **how**, can be expanded into several smaller components, including steps a student can take to complete the assignment, clearly defined learning goals or skills that will be practiced, and transparent assessment criteria.

In addition to the content of your assignment description, the way you design it and present it can also impact student success. A successful assignment is reader friendly, with built-in visual cues and formatting that allow screen readers to navigate the document. This is a crucial component of accessibility, discussed more in the following, but also discussed in greater detail in the chapter on Engagement.

Assignments and Accessibility

Accessibility in a course hinges on a student's understanding of how they will be assessed, and the support they receive toward that assessment. Determining student level of understanding in terms of assessment is predicated entirely on our ability as professional communicators: We have to:

1. say what we need them to do (assignment/activity guidelines)
2. provide support/practice for the said guidelines (resources, office hours, examples)
3. articulate what is being assessed in student-centered language (rubrics or evaluation criteria)
4. adhere to the assessment guidelines we have established (grading and feedback practices).

Deviation from any one of these four principles asks students to intuit what we want them to do/learn and ultimately sets them up for failure. Clarity issues aside, what we also know is that some students understand our assignments better than others, for a myriad of reasons, some of which we have little control over. Some students are adept at filling in the blanks we often unintentionally leave in our assignment design. The term "hidden curriculum" was first coined by Philip W. Jackson (1968), referring to the implicit messages students learn as they move through their educational phases. Since then, scholars have become keenly aware that traditional teaching methods, those narrowly centered around Western, white, and ableist cultures, leave too many students behind (Birdwell & Bayley, 2022; Daniel et al., 2022).

Students outside of these privileged groups inevitably fall into patterns of "fake it til you make it," or outright failure, neither of which support learning in a way that is transferable.

In this way, access for all students means that we must, with great intention, write and design assignments that support the various learning pathways, preferences, and needs of all students. It's a daunting task, no doubt, but the good news is that it is possible, and the rewards come in the form of broad student success through your assignments, and more importantly, through your course. One immensely helpful – albeit sometimes uncomfortable approach toward exposing these gaps in our assignment design – is to seek feedback from students. Think about it, if you want to know what users think, you must ask them. For example, if a game developer wants to conduct usability testing on the latest Souls game, they must go directly to that target audience for an accurate gauge of their software. A Souls gamer expects increasing difficulty of boss fights, the inevitable death and sometimes loss of "gather souls" and loot resources, but they also expect to learn from the mistakes of a boss battle fought one too many times over. Likewise, we as teachers must involve our target audience, students, in any inquiry toward fully understanding how they read and interpret our assignments. Students come to our classes with very specific expectations of what your class should look like, so inattention to their expectations can create deficits in understanding and content application.

Thinking in terms of our classes, students often come with several frameworks that are somewhat stable across disciplines: the teacher knows best (in theory), the teacher controls my grade, the teacher is responsible for teaching me, the teacher will tell me what I need to do, and the teacher will tell me when I am wrong. The degree of success for each one of these expectations depends heavily on how you design the course and how willing students are to engage with you and the course content. But where you can make this reciprocal engagement easier is designing assignments with multiple modality descriptions (e.g. screencasts, narration, reviewing the information in class, slides presentation), offering supporting resources and examples, incorporating a physical document (or LMS assignment description) that balances images, shaping blocking, headers, and text, and finally asking students "Does this work for you?" Sometimes the answer will be a resounding yes, and that's wonderful. Other times it might be "What the hell – and can you please tell me what I am supposed to do again?" Another way to think about your assignment's success: Do you tend to get a lot of questions about what students need to do? If the answer is yes, then likely it's time to go back to the drawing board of your assignment description and perhaps even the resources and assessment parameters.

Once you have feedback from your students – and this can certainly be informal – making the necessary revisions or starting from scratch does require a lot of time, dedication, and effort. It is not a task meant for you to complete all in one sitting or even in one semester's course. Instead, we encourage you to follow the modeling in the "Methods and Application" section, beginning first with Writing Assignment Descriptions. Beyond the descriptions themselves, it's up to you if it makes sense to then determine whether the section on "Making Your Evaluation Criteria Visible" or perhaps "Gauging Assignment Difficulty" would be more appropriate. In any case, starting with a solid, descriptive, student-centric language assignment that is also concise is the ideal place to start. And again, the only true way to gauge "student-centric language" is to ask the students themselves.

Methods and Application

Writing Assignment Descriptions

As we discussed previously, the only way to know whether your assignment is written from a student perspective is to consult them. If you're hoping to find a magic bullet for writing assignments, we don't have one. There isn't one. As subject matter experts, we are trained and become immersed in academic discourse. Writing to student audiences is a major shift, one that takes a lot of practice to master. Having said that, we all have to start somewhere, and when you are introducing an untested assignment or are tasked with developing a new course, there are a few simple guidelines that scholars agree will make that first iteration of your assignment as accessible as a first round can be (see Middleton & Reiff, 1985; Nilson, 2010; Bean, 2011; Hewett, 2015).

- Consider the course level and use appropriate disciplinary language. If your students are freshmen, you must work them toward building a disciplinary vocabulary, but even for upper-level students, consider defining complex concepts and terms to fill in gaps of understanding that may linger from their previous experiences.
- Explain the purpose of the assignment. Help students understand why they are learning these skills and how they fit into the larger context of your course.
- Clarify *how* you are assessing and *what* you are assessing in the assignment.
- Break the assignment down into smaller chunks or steps, a checklist for students to work through.

expectations is to have clear alignment between assignment instructions and assessment. If, for example, you are having students write a reflection on their most recent chemistry exam, you might ask them to include citations from lecture notes, but when you go to grade the assignment, you actually aren't concerned with citations and are instead looking at the quality of the reflection and their grasp of what they still need to work on for the next test. In this case, the guidelines shouldn't include instructions that require citations because it actually isn't what you are looking for in the assessment.

The key to learning is feedback, and this feedback must be aligned with what you actually ask students to do (Havnes et al., 2012; TILT Higher Ed Examples and Resources, 2015; Melzer, 2023). All students need continuous feedback on their progress, but if you are commenting on aspects that you didn't explicitly outline in both the guidelines and the assessment criteria, you are setting students up for failure at worst, or subpar work at best. This is another area where we, as subject matter experts and seasoned learners, find it difficult to see things from a student perspective. The truth is that we sometimes don't know what we're assessing for until we get to the assessment phase, especially for a new assignment or course. This isn't a criticism; it's more a reflection of the cyclical nature of teaching and learning. The old saying that the teacher learns more than the student is true, and we'll take that one step further and add that more often than not an instructor doesn't fully understand an assignment until after students have submitted. We say all this to illustrate that without clarity as to what you're assessing, your feedback will be arbitrary and may actually undermine the learning goals of your assignments.

There are several methods for mitigating this gap, some of which are discussed in other sections of this book. You might revisit the "Course Mapping" or "Content Development" chapters in particular. Both of these chapters ask you to think about overall course design as an interconnected activity that requires full engagement from students and instructors. Yet, for this level of collaboration to work within a classroom, assignments and assessments have to matter; they have to build on one another and have an articulable goal that is transferable beyond the course. If any of these elements are absent, we, unfortunately, are asking students to complete busy work. And we are creating more busy work for ourselves by offering feedback on assignments that have no real meaning within the course design, which takes our valuable time away from other activities we might need to provide more support on. We have to be judicious with our time and our students' time, and again this is where course mapping and content development can help us ask some hard questions about what truly matters in our courses and what does not.

This work is challenging, especially given how close we become to our assignments and course development. It can be downright painful, in fact. However, we would like to encourage you to start to think about your evaluation criteria in terms of three or four more generalizable goals. For example, Cat rather sheepishly admits she used to assess her first-year writing course assignments in a willy-nilly fashion. In other words, she often found herself halfway through a stack of papers before she realized what she was actually grading for. The truth is all of us have done some level of this type of assessment in our courses, but we want to challenge you to spend your time articulating three or four major goals for each assignment. Nowadays, Cat hones in on three or four clear goals for each feedback stage of a larger assignment movement. For example, in her writing assignments, she might emphasize that on their first draft students are practicing the three goals of (1) synthesizing sources, (2) incorporating quotations, and (3) building a reference list. This means that during the feedback for that draft, Cat will give each student feedback on their progress toward assessment for those three goals. She also offers feedback as needed to students who have other gaps, but this approach of three clear goals helps Cat streamline her feedback process, and it enables every student to revise toward the same assessment goals.

Assessing Your Evaluation Criteria

As we've suggested previously, evaluation criteria informs what and how you assess student work. So while it's true that students learn much more than we can capture in any one assessment, and the goal of higher education should not be limited to just measuring how well a student performs, assessment can be a tool for good or ill, depending on how well it's applied. Put more succinctly, no matter what your personal goals are for your students, if your instruction and feedback do not align with your assessment, your students will falter.

A common refrain from students of all ages and abilities is that sometimes instructors expect them to know or perform things in assignments that they've never been taught.

For this reason, we recommend that you spend some time *assessing your assessment* methods:

- Are you teaching what you're assessing?
- Are you assessing what you're teaching?
- Are you clarifying to students what you're assessing?

- Are you providing resources that scaffold what you are assessing?
- Are you making visible to students what you are assessing both in the guidelines and the evaluation criteria?

Model in Practice

Our models in this section are a little different than what you might expect for assignment guidelines recommendations. Rather than simply replicating a series of questions or prompts to help you develop prompts, we have opted to provide a combination of design, accessibility, and development advice. For some, it may be more helpful to think about layout and design elements like white space and leveled headings; for others, a targeted approach on your evaluation criteria may be more useful. In any case, like the rest of our book, where you spend your time is up to you. And if you are newer to this process or have been given carte blanche to develop your course from scratch, we would recommend thinking through what you want to evaluate first, then consider design and specific guideline criteria.

Accessible Design Elements

While there are many design elements to consider when developing assignment guidelines, we have found that two key elements are essential: the use of heading styles and white space. Both provide maximum accessibility in such a way that it goes beyond traditional ADA compliance, ultimately benefiting all users regardless of their learning needs and preferences (Figure 2.1).

Visual Supports

Let's get real – for some teacher-designers, visuals and artsy type stuff just ain't their thing. And that's okay. That said, do not underestimate the power of visual rhetoric and its ability to communicate meaning in a way that alphanumeric text cannot. Screencasts, for example, have offered the option of a student being walked through the assignment and resources with the instructor. The teacher can highlight important text with a cursor and demonstrate assignment skills, while the student can choose to pause the video at any point. Likewise, still images might provide illustrative models or help to break up the text heaviness of an assignment so that it is much easier to read on a screen (Figure 2.2).

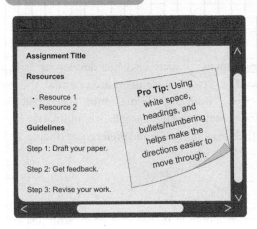

Figure 2.1 Models for using heading styles and white space that allow for greater ease of audience engagement

Evaluation Criteria

We have all had that moment where we think we are telling students what they need to do for a project only to find out that isn't ultimately what we are assessing for. Articulating what we want to be able to assess is perhaps

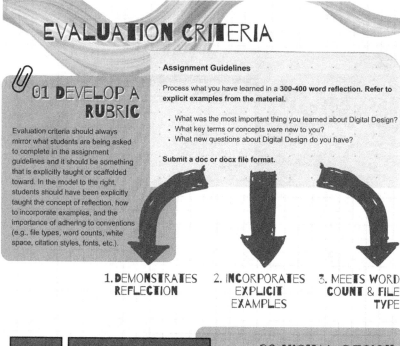

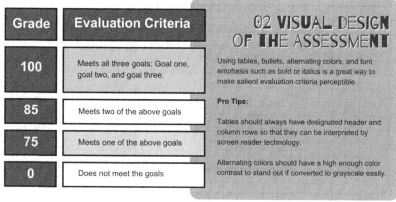

Figure 2.2 Importance of visual design elements such as screencasts and images, which assist in students' understanding of the assignment expectations

the most important first step to designing accessible guidelines. Such criteria must also be written in a manner easy for the student to follow, and it must be visually designed in such a way that it helps students understand what is being asked of them (Figure 2.3).

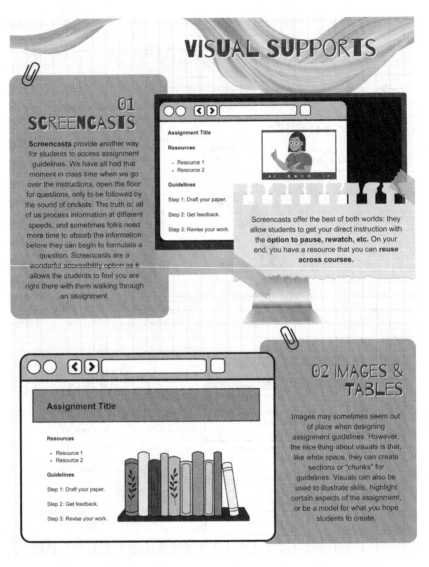

Figure 2.3 How to determine what an assignment is assessing with suggestions of how to represent the evaluation criteria visually.

Writing Accessible Guidelines

For us, our background in rhetoric and writing can sometimes mean that we can be slightly verbose. And in an effort to fully explain our point, our meaning might get lost along the way. When we think about writing accessible guidelines, we have to think about the language level, use of bullets and numbering, and integration of intra, inter, and external-course resources (Figure 2.4). For more on this topic, we recommend you revisit the "Scaffolding" chapter.

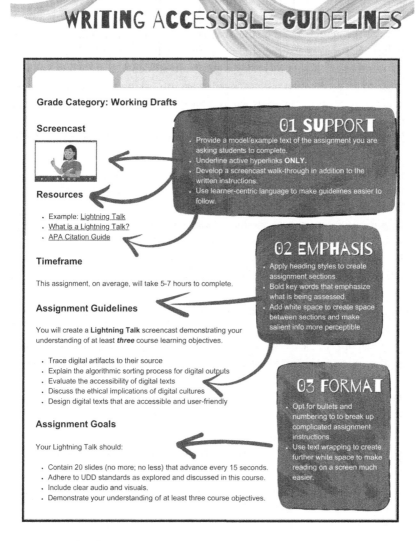

Figure 2.4 A brief annotated assignment example, noting the elements that make guidelines maximally accessible to learners

Putting Your Layers Together

Let's get real for a second – or perhaps for the fifteenth time in this book – the three of us as teacher/scholar/designers, have a lot of answers and solutions, but by no means do we have them all. Instead, we hope that this chapter has challenged you to consider methods, approaches, and questions you might ask yourself when designing assignments for your classes. Key among this process is not divorcing assignment descriptions from resources or assessments or the actual layout of the assignment instructions itself. These are all part of what makes a successful assignment, which can only be determined by a number of factors including input from students. Even when students appear to do well with a project, it still warrants asking them how the guidelines and supporting materials worked for them in the process. You may find that you have done a stellar job in crafting the ultimate assignment, or you may learn that students wound up using many other supplemental materials that are external to your course. Granted, you can congratulate their ingenuity, but you can also take this as a potential opportunity for you to incorporate some of the resources that informed their work and maybe even consider adjusting your assignment design accordingly.

If we could impart only one bit of wisdom from this chapter above all else it would be this: you have to get student input. All of your assumptions about what works best for students is an amazing starting point, but if you don't get input from your end-user (the students), issues of success and sustainability will inevitably rise. Students as well as colleagues you can collaborate with are the ultimate resource when it comes to developing a course design that has real impact beyond the scope of just one semester/year/quarter. And if we are willing to treat our course design work as an ever-evolving iterative process, we open ourselves up to providing a learning experience that is truly accessible for all.

Checklist

- [ ] Writing assignments from the student perspective. Consider the course level and use appropriate language.
- [ ] Explain the purpose of the assignment and its relevance to the course.
- [ ] Clarify the assessment criteria and expectations.
- [ ] Break down the assignment into smaller chunks or steps, creating a checklist for students.
- [ ] Design assignments with multiple pathways to support different learning styles and preferences.
- [ ] Assess your assessment methods to ensure they align with the feedback you offer and what you teach.

References and Resources

Al-Abyadh, M. H. A., & Azeem, H. A. H. A. (2022). Academic achievement: Influences of university students' self-management and perceived self-efficacy. *Journal of Intelligence*, *10*(3), 55. https://doi.org/10.3390/jintelligence10030055

Bean, J. C. (2011). *Engaging ideas: The professor's guide to integrating writing, critical thinking, and active learning in the classroom*. Hoboken, NJ: Jossey-Bass.

Birdwell, M. L. N., & Bayley, K. (2022). Feature: When the syllabus is ableist: Understanding how class policies fail disabled students. *Teaching English in the Two-Year College*, *49*(3), 220–237. https://doi.org/10.58680/tetyc202231803

Curum, B., & Khedo, K. K. (2021). Cognitive load management in mobile learning systems: Principles and theories. *Journal of Computers in Education (the Official Journal of the Global Chinese Society for Computers in Education)*, *8*(1), 109–136. https://doi.org/10.1007/s40692-020-00173-6

Daniel, J. R., Malcolm, K., & Rai, C. (Eds.). (2022). *Writing across difference: Theory and intervention*. Logan, UT: Utah State University Press.

Havnes, A., Smith, K., Dysthe, O., & Ludvigsen, K. (2012). Formative assessment and feedback: Making learning visible. *Studies in Educational Evaluation*, *38*(1), 21–27. https://doi.org/10.1016/j.stueduc.2012.04.001

Hewett, B. (2015). *Reading to learn and writing to teach: Literacy strategies for online writing instruction*. London: Macmillan Higher Education.

Jackson, P. W. (1968). *Life in classrooms*. New York, NY: Teachers College Press.

Kuh, G. D., Kinzie, J., Buckley, J., Bridges, B. K., & Hayek, J. C. (2006). *What matters to student success: A review of the literature*. National Postsecondary Education Cooperative. Retrieved from https://nces.ed.gov/npec/pdf/kuh_team_report.pdf

MacNaul, H., Garcia, R., Cividini-Motta, C., & Thacker, I. (2021). Effect of assignment choice on student academic performance in an online class. *Behavior Analysis in Practice*, *14*(4), 1074–1078. https://doi.org/10.1007/s40617-021-00566-8

Melzer, D. (2023). *Reconstructing response to student writing: A national study from across the curriculum*. Logan, UT: Utah State UP.

Middleton, J. E., & Reiff, J. D. (1985). A "Student-Based" approach to writing assignments. *College Composition and Communication*, *36*(2), 232–234. https://doi.org/10.2307/357444

Muniz, J., Fernandez-Alonso, R., Suarez-Alvarez, J., & Alvarez-Diaz, M. (2017). Students' achievement and homework assignment strategies. *Frontiers in Psychology*, *8*, 286–286. https://doi.org/10.3389/fpsyg.2017.00286

Nilson, L. B. (2010). *Teaching at its best: A research-based resource for college instructors* (3rd ed.). Hoboken, NJ: Jossey-Bass.

Skulmowski, A., & Xu, K. M. (2022). Understanding cognitive load in digital and online learning: A new perspective on extraneous cognitive load. *Educational Psychology Review*, *34*(1), 171–196. https://doi.org/10.1007/s10648-021-09624-7

TILT Higher Ed Examples and Resources. (2015, September 2). Retrieved September 20, 2023, from https://tilthighered.com/tiltexamplesandresources

York, T. T., Gibson, C., & Rankin, S. (2015). Defining and measuring academic success. *Practical Assessment, Research & Evaluation*, *20*, 5.

Engagement

3

Introduction/Overview

It might not seem evident at first why we include a whole chapter on engagement in a course design manual, but we have come to learn that running an engaging course happens only through thoughtful and intentional design. Engagement is not an aspect of the course that exists in the ether; instead, it is an opportunity to view course content as a critical mechanism for engaging students. Often, it is too easy for us to get hung up on the notion that engagement is solely transactional in nature, and only occurs student-to-student, student-to-teacher, or teacher-to-students plural. All the instructor presence and personality pizazz in the world cannot and will not make up for course design and material that is inaccessible, confusing, and cannot clearly articulate a specific learning goal. This is where revisiting the sections on Gauging Assignment Difficulty and Assessing Your Evaluation Criteria in the "Assignments" chapter, and the discussion of learning goals from the "Scaffolding" chapter would be useful. These sections offer specific questions for not only gauging assignment relevance, learning goals, and assessment criteria, but such work also exposes potential opportunities to create student motivation. Let's be honest: getting a pass/fail or alpha-numeric score for a class is not enough motivation for students to complete work in such a way that the content is transferable beyond academic contexts. As teachers, we are tasked with creating a more immersive model of learning that positions our course content as concepts/practices that have real impact. The weight of this responsibility is not lost on us as teacher-scholars, so it is with this mindset that we invite you to think of engagement as motivation not only on the part of students, but on you as the instructor as well.

DOI: 10.4324/9781003485476-4

Knowing what best motivates individuals in a classroom setting takes a good bit of trial and error to tease out what works best for any one instructor in any given context. Another key concern is what to do when things don't go as planned. Consider that COVID caused disruption due to a lack of understanding of broader ways to facilitate engagement for students. The pandemic and all of its horrific consequences both in and outside the classroom began to push us to consider what really motivates us, hence the mass exodus from many workplaces that were on some level not fulfilling. In the spirit of not wanting our students to "quietly quit" from the confines of our courses, this chapter offers strategies for engagement across teaching modalities (f2f, online, and hybrid). In particular, we explore ways of enhancing student participation in virtual modalities, including ways to foster instructor-student interaction and instructor outreach to enhance students' sense of belonging and inclusion. Notice that our goal here is not to create a one-way interchange between the instructor and students. Instead, our models and questions throughout this chapter ask us to consider our classrooms as complicated intersections with overpasses and underpasses that do not always need the mediation of the teacher.

What Is Engagement?

Engagement refers to the level of motivation and genuine interest a student has toward a task, assignment, or overall course. Some of this, of course, depends on the student's disposition, but there are strategies instructors can use to enhance or hinder engagement.

Let's start by thinking about what engagement looks like. Engaged students actively participate and take ownership of their learning. They set goals and monitor their own progress to reach their own predetermined notion of success (Lowenthal & Wilson, 2010). Engaged students ask questions, seek collaboration, and use available resources. They want to learn and are okay with making mistakes. As we've already pointed out, this is a disposition that students bring to a learning context, but because college classes are taken across a multi-year system, what happens in any individual class can nurture engagement or push students toward disengagement. In other words, what happens in our classes matters, even though it's just one of many that students will move through.

Here's why we should care about nurturing engagement: research shows that engagement is a solid predictor of academic success (Chen et al., 2010; Bautista et al., 2019; Richardson et al., 2019), and higher engagement has been correlated to stronger social and emotional skills in students (Dymnicki et al., 2016). And there is ample research about how to increase engagement that can inform how we design our classes. For example, scholars point toward key factors that impact engagement: (1) **course design** (layout, organization, usability, clarity), (2) **meaningful learning experiences** (group projects, discussions, problem-solving tasks), and (3) **interactive learning tools** (discussion forums, simulations, multimedia resources, collaborative tools) (Swan, 2001). In addition, the way we present content to students through the learning management system (LMS) can impact student engagement. Scholars emphasize the need to **make design visible** and **invite students to view themselves as co-creators and co-designers** of an online course (Harris & Greer, 2017).

Engagement and Accessibility

Returning to the intersection metaphor discussed in the overview, we would like for you to pause for a moment and consider what happens to classroom motivation when all interactions are mitigated by the instructor. Think of it this way: teacher-to-class interactions are only like a left-hand-turn traffic light that doesn't dependably offer a green turn arrow. Those already in the street, the first come–first served if you will, can use the traffic laws just as intended – they will turn left when the signal allows. These lucky few at the beginning of the line are much like students who know how to "play the game" of school; the knowledge they learn in your class may not be retained, but they know enough about how to behave as students to be successful. Others that aren't yet able to move up in the queue because of a poorly timed signal are stuck overlapping into the straight lane or the median, causing potential dangers for other drivers. These drivers are similar to students who are stumped and waiting for an opportunity to get direct instructor intervention, and if the opportunity never comes, or if peer-to-peer engagement opportunities aren't built into the class, these students may quit altogether. The third set of potential drivers might be less inclined to stay put and instead opt for a workaround. Ever resilient, they go down the road, make a U-Turn, return to the intersection, and exit right as this opposite lane has an extended green. These folks might be similar to students who don't like asking questions and opt for answers elsewhere, like their peers or YouTube videos, which may or may not be in their best interest in terms of doing well in the course. The common element for all this trouble? The left-hand traffic light. This light – and we all know that intersection where this is true – could be likened to teachers who only design their courses as *instructor-centric* rather than *student-centric*.

On the one hand, the onus to be on your game every day means you are functioning similarly to the aforementioned traffic light that is letting some through, stopping others, and forcing others to resort to additional labor to do well. Sole authority to lead the class, deposit knowledge as Freire (1972/2007) would say, is left to us. Over time, our motivation to keep this pace up will wane, and students will likely give up their own motivations to learn the content for more than just a grade. On the other hand, creating that space where engagement is more than just a grade is up to us – not by controlling the class from a top-down approach – but rather by building in thoughtful entry points for discussion, collaboration, and meaning-making that are both challenging and rewarding at the same time.

The most important connection between engagement and accessibility is **motivation**. If students aren't invested in their own learning, they gain less content knowledge overall and realize only minimal growth in their critical thinking skills. This is where revisiting the "Scaffolding" chapter may be of benefit. Considering your coursework flow, what assignments really do build toward larger course outcomes? What assignments are merely items to help a student practice for a larger goal or capstone? When you answer these two questions, think from the student's perspective – do they see this assignment/ activity as building to a larger objective or as a mode of practice? If the answer is "no," the problem may be the activity is actually busy work (we all do that on some level), or perhaps there is a transparency issue where students can't extrapolate from your guidelines what the "point" or "purpose" is. This is ultimately an opportunity to articulate an assignment purpose, and even just a small move like this can have maximum results with minimum effort on your part as the instructor.

Back to the point about busy work, when we discover it – or perhaps more accurately, when we come to a place where we can accept it and name it – we have yet another opportunity to give space to regain motivation for you and your students. Sometimes it is okay to do nothing. Let that sink in. Yes, we said that sometimes it is okay to do nothing. Mental health can and absolutely is an accessibility issue; when we are overworked, mentally and physically tired, or our brains are just too damned cluttered, processing and thinking critically in a classroom space becomes much more difficult. Offer an in-class workday, or if your institutional structures allow, schedule an asynchronous workday if you are in-person or synchronous online, giving students the flexibility to work on whatever major task they have in the queue. It's not always necessary to do this work under the teacher's nose or at the set time of the class. Your students can take some agency to work ahead, then use the class time to sleep in, binge-watch the latest streaming show, or perhaps complete other pressing coursework. From your perspective, you have bought yourself time as well. Maybe you need the class time to catch up on responding to student work, or perhaps a home project you have been putting off. Learning happens when people are motivated, and motivation comes as a part of a balanced approach to a work-life both in and outside of the class. That said, we cannot account for every issue of motivation for students since the contributing factors are complicated and personal. But that doesn't mean we shouldn't consider this aspect of our teaching as much as any other aspects discussed in this manual. And the good news is that no matter your course content, there are a variety of best practices to choose from to fit your teaching style and instructional goals.

Another accessibility concern relates to **tools of engagement**. While we have myriad digital platforms that purport to enhance student engagement, we caution instructors not to fall into a trap of adopting a new shiny online quiz or game app simply because it looks fun. There's no reason learning can't be "fun," but this is a good time to emphasize our overall message: accessible learning is not a one-size-fits-all approach. To ensure that all students can succeed, you must offer a variety of engaging formats to ensure access for all types of learners. This includes incorporating various formats like text, images, audio, and video, to cater to different learning preferences and accommodate learners with sensory differences, and providing alt-text descriptions, captions, transcripts, and audio descriptions for multimedia content.

One of the greatest challenges, especially in online teaching modalities, is fostering peer-to-peer **collaboration and interaction**, an essential component of deep learning and knowledge-making. The classroom climate you establish and the tools you choose for group work and peer feedback can either greatly enhance or greatly hinder access for different learners. Providing accessible communication tools, accommodating different communication styles, and offering alternatives for participation (e.g., written contributions instead of live discussions) can make interactions inclusive and engaging for all learners.

Methods and Application

Students as Co-Creators

As we've already mentioned, student success is directly connected to how much they care and are invested in their own learning. In one of Cat's recent student evaluations, a first-year writing student noted that some of the assignments were too simple, which led them to rush through and submit with minimal effort. This student was self-aware enough to understand that the potential growth they could have gained by more fully engaging was not realized because of their lack of investment and labor in their own learning. In this same batch of course evaluations, several other students expressed a sense of feeling overwhelmed and unable to keep up with the demanding pace of the course, but that they had learned a lot. We share this example because it's not unusual to have such different experiences within the same class cohort. It's another area that makes teaching complicated and anything but straightforward.

One of the key ways of getting students to invest in their learning is to empower them, to allow them opportunities to set their own learning goals and to tailor class projects toward their interests. When their learning experiences are meaningful and relevant to their lives, they make connections to real-world applications and begin to see the practical value of what they are learning. In addition, when it's feasible, giving students opportunities to choose the digital tools and genres they use for their classwork can also be a way to spark engagement, especially when they understand how learning to use such tools will benefit them in future professional and academic pursuits.

Another way to encourage motivation is to help students recognize their learning and growth through reflective self-assessments. Consider that one of the goals of education is to foster a sense of lifelong learning, so helping students build good habits of self-reflection that encourage them to evaluate their own effort and effectiveness of their study habits provides them important critical thinking skills for all future contexts. It can also help students understand their strengths and prepare them for self-advocacy in later learning situations.

Fostering Peer-to-Peer Collaboration

Sometimes when a student expresses confusion, Cat will ask another student who understands to explain it to their classmate. This almost always works, and it serves multiple purposes. First, it builds trust between students, an essential component of peer review or peer evaluation. Second, it helps students recognize that the instructor is not the only source of support in a classroom. Finally, it encourages students to learn from each other, and this sharing of the knowledge-making process leads to deeper understanding overall.

Establishing this sense of trust and support across classmates early in a course will also set your students up for success in group projects. Group work promotes social connections and allows students to engage in meaningful interactions that enhance their understanding of course content, as well as a deeper awareness of the variety of ways that learning occurs across different cultures and value systems.

To add another layer of accountability and reflection, some instructors find it helpful to allow students to assess, evaluate, or offer feedback to group members on how well they perform as collaborators. This is especially effective in larger classes where instructors can't logistically manage groups in any close way. You can consider making such evaluations anonymous to avoid group conflicts, and you can choose to consider these evaluations as part of a student's overall grade or simply let it serve as a tool for self-reflection.

The Importance of Instructor Presence

One semester, Cat had a student approach her after class one day. His head was low and he seemed embarrassed. He spilled out an awkward apology for submitting several assignments late and for, as he put it, letting Cat down by his subpar performance. Cat reassured him that she understood his struggle to manage the workload of being a new college student. He exhaled and seemed visibly grateful. After a bit more discussion, it became clear that this student felt a connection with Cat as his instructor and was concerned about disappointing her. She reassured him that his performance would not impact her opinion of him on a personal level, nor does she judge students based on any perception of where her class falls in a student's list of priorities. We share this story as a way to understand how students view their relationships with instructors, and what happens when students feel connected to a course. For some, this is another aspect of teaching that takes effort and practice, especially for those who feel more awkward or have less confidence in the classroom. On the other end of the spectrum are those who open up too much, struggling to maintain proper boundaries, which can lead to a host of concerns. Cat tends to fall into the latter category, and sometimes she has students who share inappropriate personal information, and this has only gotten worse since COVID.

The larger point here is that research supports the effectiveness of getting to know your students and showing genuine interest in their learning (Deslauriers et al., 2019; Amerstorfer, 2020; Amerstorfer & Freiin von Münster-Kistner, 2021). When students sense that you care about them and their success in your course, their motivation and engagement increases. But we've seen instructors struggle, as Cat does, with being too open.

It's More Than Just the Tool (It's What You Do With the Tools)

There's a reason the educational market is inundated with apps, websites, and other digital tools. They're fun. They're easy. They're versatile. They can also become crutches, and worse, if you don't choose the right tool, or if you bombard students with too many tools, their learning is actually diminished.

We encourage you to consider the following guidelines when selecting tools for engagement:

- What do students gain by learning to use the tool? Is it more than just a fun way to engage students? Choose tools that allow students to create digital products and practice digital literacies, helping them build transferable skills.
- What is the learning curve for the tool? Some digital tools may be too complex or not user-friendly, which can lead to disengagement and frustration among students.
- Do students need to have personal accounts to use the tool? Be cautious of digital tools that may compromise student privacy or data.
- Are there levels of access based on which students can afford a paid subscription?

Model in Practice

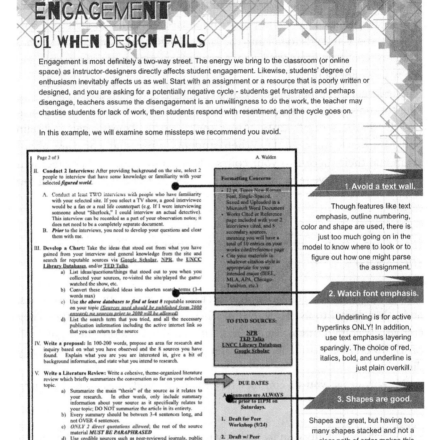

Figure 3.1 When Design Fails

ENGAGEMENT
02 WHEN INSTRUCTIONS FAIL

Cat and Ashlyn are both writing and design teachers, and as such, the level of detail in assignment explanations can vary. Cat errs on the side of shorter descriptions that follow the guidelines of technical writing. Ashlyn, however, tends to overexplain. While both have their merits, a meeting in the middle is ideal - keeping an eye out for simplicity and directness while still offering enough information to help students be successful.

In the examples below, we will explore some of the pitfalls of assignment instructions.

1. Avoid needless repetitiveness.

Extra instructional information is not always necessary. "Only two direct quotes" implies that the rest must be paraphrased. Likewise, noting the summary of each source is 3-4 sentences means don't go over 4.

V. **Write a Literature Review:** Write a cohesive, theme-organized literature review which briefly summarizes the conversation so far on your selected topic.

 a) Summarize the main "thesis" of the source as it relates to your research. In other words, only include summary information about your source as it specifically relates to your topic; DO NOT summarize the article in its entirety.
 b) Every summary should be between 3-4 sentences long, and not OVER 4 sentences.
 c) ONLY 2 direct quotations allowed; the rest of the source material MUST BE PARAPHRASED
 d) Use credible sources such as peer-reviewed journals, public radio segments, & TED Talk presentations.
 e) Parenthetical or footnoted citations should be throughout this section depending on the citation style.

Notations like parenthetical or footnoted citations are not needed. To say that you need to use a particular citation style means that such instructions will be internal to the citation information guides and aren't necessary on the assignment sheet. The explanation in the right-hand box would be a better way to state this requirement in the assignment sheet.

• Cite your materials in whatever citation style is appropriate for your intended major (IEEE, MLA, APA, Chicago-Turabian, etc.)

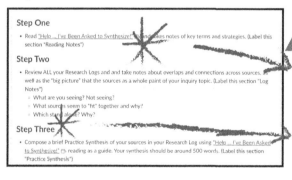

Step One
• Read "Help ... I've Been Asked to Synthesize!" and takes notes of key terms and strategies. (Label this section "Reading Notes")

Step Two
• Review ALL your Research Logs and and take notes about overlaps and connections across sources, as well as the "big picture" that the sources as a whole paint of your inquiry topic. (Label this section "Log Notes")
 ◦ What are you seeing? Not seeing?
 ◦ What sources seem to "fit" together and why?
 ◦ Which stand alone? Why?

Step Three
• Compose a brief Practice Synthesis of your sources in your Research Log using "Help ... I've Been Asked to Synthesize!" reading as a guide. Your synthesis should be around 500 words. (Label this section "Practice Synthesis")

2. Expanding and providing examples is a must.

Though clear, concise, and direct, the absence of a model may make this work more inaccessible.

Sometimes an assignment can benefit from extending it into several smaller activities. In later iterations, Cat expanded the instruction and practice for synthesis.

Figure 3.2 When Instructions Fail

ENGAGEMENT

03 WHEN DESIGN & GUIDELINES ARE ON POINT

Developing a design for an assignment or activity that is ideal and works for students takes time, practice, and input from students/colleagues. Materials that are created well with attentiveness to accessibility will offer multiple means of engagement, clearly labeled sections, font emphasis, and alt text as needed.

This example extends Cat's original synthesis assignment, which she developed over many semesters with the help of students, colleagues, and her own developing knowledge in design.

Add a Heading 2 that says **Practice Synthesis**

Under this heading 2, write a Practice Synthesis of about 200 words that focuses on **one theme** you **see across at least 3 of your sources** in your Research Log.

Here are further things you should consider:

1. Explain the theme you identified clearly and thoroughly. The paragraph should focus on this theme. Use your sources as evidence/examples to help you discuss this theme.
2. Make sure each source is introduced individually by name, and add a hyperlinked title within the text.
3. Avoid using redundant, basic language like "the first source," "the second source," etc. Instead, practice higher level prose styles.
4. Avoid discussing one source, then moving on to the next. Draw connections between your sources and their ideas. Your job is to weave them together so your reader clearly sees how these sources are intertwined, and how they discuss the same idea in different ways.
5. Include quotes from sources as appropriate. Practice incorporating quotes into your own sentence.

For more help with this assignment, review the Anatomy of a Synthesis page.

NOTE: You must submit your log on time to be part of the Peer Response activity for your Practice Synthesis.

Instructions are expanded with description but are by no means overkill.

Features like font emphasis, numbering, leveled headings, shape, and high contrast are used.

Some students are able to follow the expectations of assignment guidelines easily. Others need an example. This revised version includes an annotated example to walk students through synthesizing.

Figure 3.3 When Design and Guidelines are on Point

Putting Your Layers Together

Ultimately, we want to encourage you to consider engagement as not only part of your active teaching presence but also part of your overall course design. Engagement is more complicated than just holding students' attention or choosing the newest gizmo. If this is an area you feel needs more attention or guidance than we've offered, you could consider consulting a colleague you know has proven success or confidence in keeping students engaged to find out what they can recommend. We've found that it comes more naturally to some instructors than others. Having said that, we are all different, and it's not our job to "entertain" students or feel responsible for their own lack of motivation about a topic or class focus.

To reiterate one last time, we only have so much power or control over the individual experiences of students. Focus on what you can do and don't let anyone's lack of interest disrupt what you know to be valuable and appropriate for your teaching.

Checklist

- ☐ Incorporate various formats (text, images, audio, video) to cater to different learning preferences. This might include audio descriptions of visual content, video walkthroughs of written assignments, etc.
- ☐ Offer alternatives for participation. For example, allowing written contributions for learners who struggle to participate in live discussions.
- ☐ Clearly communicate and provide guidance for expectations for respectful and inclusive interactions, including peer-to-peer and student-to-instructor interactions.
- ☐ Establish a pathway/system for students to offer feedback and make necessary adjustments to improve engagement over time.
- ☐ Consider offering videos or tutorials to support learners in navigating your course site and your assignments effectively. This also enhances instructor presence, especially in online modalities.

References and Resources

Amerstorfer C. M. (2020). Problem-based learning for preservice teachers of English as a foreign language. *Colloquium: New Philologies, 5*, 75–90. 10.23963/cnp.2020.5.1.4

Amerstorfer, C. M., & Freiin von Münster-Kistner, C. (2021). Student perceptions of academic engagement and student-teacher relationships in problem-based learning. *Frontiers in Psychology, 12*, 713057–713057. https://doi.org/10.3389/fpsyg.2021.713057

Bautista, J. R., Bautista, J. A., & Bautista, J. M. (2019). Student engagement and academic performance of students of Partido State University. *Journal of Education and Practice, 10*(3), 1–9.

Borgman, J., & McArdle, C. (Eds.). (2019). *Personal, accessible, responsive, strategic: Resources and strategies for online writing instructors.* Fort Collins, CO: WAC Clearinghouse.

Borgman, J., & McArdle, C. (Eds.). (2021). *PARS in practice: More resources and strategies for online writing instructors.* Fort Collins, CO: WAC Clearinghouse.

Chen, Y., Lambert, A. D., & Guidry, K. R. (2010). The effects of student engagement, student satisfaction, and perceived learning in online learning environments. *International Journal on E-Learning, 9*(3), 325–340.

Deslauriers, L., McCarty, L. S., Miller, K., Callaghan, K., & Kestin, G. (2019). Measuring actual learning versus feeling of learning in response to being actively engaged in the classroom. *Proceedings of the National Academy of Sciences – PNAS, 116*(39), 19251–19257. https://doi.org/10.1073/pnas.1821936116

Dymnicki, A., Sambolt, M., & Osher, D. (2016). *Improving college and career readiness by incorporating social and emotional learning.* College and Career Readiness and Success Center. https://ccrscenter.org/sites/default/files/Improving%20College%20and%20Career%20Readiness%20by%20Incorporating%20Social%20and%20Emotional%20Learning_0.pdf

Freire, P. (1972/2017). *Pedagogy of the oppressed.* Penguin Books Ltd.

Harris, H., & Greer, M. (2017). Over, under, or through: Design strategies to supplement the LMS and enhance interaction in online writing courses. *Communication Design Quarterly Review, 4*(4), 46–54. https://doi.org/10.1145/3071088.3071093

Kuo, Y. C., Walker, A. E., Schroder, K. E., & Belland, B. R. (2022). Engagement in online learning: Student attitudes and behavior during COVID-19. *Computers & Education, 166*, 104181.

Lowenthal, P., & Wilson, B. G. (2010). Labels DO matter! A critique of AECT's redefinition of the field. *TechTrends, 54*(1), 38–46. https://doi.org/10.1007/s11528-009-0362-y

Richardson, J. T., Elliott, P., & Roberts, R. (2019). Student engagement and wellbeing over time at a higher education institution. *Higher Education Research & Development, 38*(5), 1026–1040.

Swan, K. (2001). Virtual interaction: Design factors affecting student satisfaction and perceived learning in asynchronous online courses. *Distance Education, 22*(2), 306–331. https://doi.org/10.1080/0158791010220208

Zhang, Y., Li, Y., Li, Y., & Li, Y. (2022). Dynamic interaction between student learning behaviour and learning environment: Meta-analysis of student engagement and its influencing factors. *Educational Research Review, 38*, 100447.

Designing for Assistive Technologies 4

Overview

This chapter explores assistive technology and the potential implications of engaging with digitally mediated course elements such as resources, assignment submissions, and group activities. Though many platforms have native accessibility checkers, the extent of success in identifying potential barriers is varied. The goal of this chapter is to help instructors identify basic practices for creating accessible course content that is attentive to assistive technology, specifically inviting them to consider how some widely used platforms, such as Google Drive, may have potential compatibility issues with certain assistive technologies like screen readers.

What Are Assistive Technologies?

For many, assistive technologies are tools designed to offset students' disabilities, enable them to perform tasks, and enhance their learning success (Akpan & Beard, 2013; Desmond et al., 2018; Chambers, 2019; Fernández-Batanero et al., 2022). Though primarily intended to aid individuals with disabilities, such accessibility features like speech-to-text, virtual assistant screen reading, and alt text hover descriptions are available to everyone and have, in fact, been useful to users who didn't have a particular barrier that warranted their use. Assistive technologies include a wide range of tools, devices, software, and equipment designed to assist users in performing tasks, overcoming challenges, and enhancing their independence (Ahmad, 2015). These technologies aim to bridge the gap between individuals – in this case, students – and

DOI: 10.4324/9781003485476-5

their environment – in this case, learning contexts. This includes any technology that helps students and instructors communicate and participate more effectively in various learning modes.

Rather than naming specific assistive technology platforms, we will talk about what they do and how they offer space for inclusion and access through three broad categories:

- Converting text to speech (e.g., screen readers)
- Converting speech to text (e.g., dictation software, closed captioning)
- Converting image to text (e.g., alt-text, closed captioning)

Assistive Tech and Accessibility

Aside from the more obvious connections, the larger point we hope to emphasize in this book is that all learners benefit from enhanced access when we design our courses to be accessible through assistive technologies. As accessibility scholars, we view assistive technology from much broader perspectives, complicating the notion of accessibility as a space between the publicly observable and internally manifested (Wilson & Lewiecki-Wilson, 2001). Access is an issue of visible and invisible barriers, meaning that identities such as class, race, gender, age, learning styles/preferences, or education level may create situations when success is limited (Mahaffey & Walden, 2019; Walden, 2022). We embrace the growing consensus among accessibility scholars that we are all temporarily abled, pushing back on ableist practices that burden offset barriers onto those who don't fit within dominant cultural views on an invulnerable body and mind (Garland-Thomson, 1997; Dolmage, 2017). In other words, we subscribe to the notion that disability is a complicated lived experience that is rarely – if ever – static (Dolmage, 2014). We hope to promote this shift in perspective toward acknowledging the temporary nature of ability.

Next, we believe that current practices in higher education of requiring students to disclose disabilities perpetuate stigma around differences (Dolmage, 2017). Designing your course for all learners, no matter their ability, creates an inclusive learning environment, making students with hidden disabilities feel valued and supported without having to request accommodations that often place undue burdens on both students and teachers (Mahaffey & Walden, 2019; Oswal & Meloncon, 2014). Thus, being proactive in creating course materials that are accessible through assistive technology welcomes your students with disabilities in ways that reactive policies fail to do. We also encourage instructors to explicitly discuss with students how their course design supports assistive technologies since this acclimates students to developing empathy and awareness of this topic, a necessary soft skill in today's professional realms.

In a similar way, accessible materials and activities accommodate various learning styles and preferences, facilitating active engagement and participation among students. When students can access content in ways that suit their individual needs, they are more likely to be actively involved in the learning process (Walden, 2022). When all students feel supported and accommodated, they are more likely to engage with your assignments and succeed in your course ... and beyond in their studies.

Methods and Application

The first step in designing for assistive technology is to develop a basic understanding of how it works. For example, screen readers rely on built-in headings and font styles to navigate and read text on a screen. If proper attention is not given to formatting an assignment or LMS page, the screen reader cannot function as well. Likewise, consider that students are accustomed to using a wide variety of tools when producing communication, including digital assistants like Alexa and Siri who dictate search terms and read and write text messages. Therefore, if you require your students to compose or create on a platform that doesn't offer speech-to-text, some students will be limited in their ability to perform.

We recommend a two-pronged approach to assistive technologies in your classroom: (1) designing your course materials so students can access them through assistive technologies; and (2) choosing platforms that allow students to use assistive technologies in creating their course products. Consider at all times that what we do in our courses serves as models for students in best practices for their personal and professional lives.

Creating Accessible Content for Assistive Technology

Let's revisit our three categories of assistive technology and consider best practices for design that facilitate their use.

First, let's consider **text-to-speech** technologies like screen readers. These rely on built-in textual elements like headings, subheadings, and page numbers. We would argue that all digital texts should adhere to such basic best practices, but certainly, course materials should be organized around leveled headings that are descriptive and clear. We caution against overreliance on PDFs that can be inaccessible, especially when readings and images are scanned through a copier. A good rule of thumb is to check your document for accessibility by copying and pasting text from one document to another. If you cannot successfully do this, or if the resulting copy/paste results in odd spacings that do not resemble the original text, you must offer this material in another format.

This is a good time to discuss what might be a bone of contention for some, that is the debate about whether listening to a text being read *is reading*. We contend that attention toward equity and inclusion pushes us toward an understanding that just because a student doesn't navigate their learning pathways in the same way earlier generations did doesn't mean they are inherently flawed (Wolf, 2018). Reading is about comprehension. Some people need to see the words to understand; others need to hear them, and still others need a combination of the two. Cat learned this firsthand as a parent. She has three children, each with very different learning preferences. Her oldest child used a method of rewriting notes as a study method; her middle child would ask her to call out questions and study materials to prepare for tests, needing to hear the content to absorb it; and her youngest child would use a system of flashcards. Ashlyn's two children, likewise, have very different reading needs as well. Her older son is autistic and hyperlexic, meaning he is an excellent reader and can often pronounce words he's never encountered before. Comprehension-wise, his reading on his own results in mixed outcomes that often do not indicate he's absorbed the material. However, when he can read a text along with a text-to-speech tool often innate in early education learning tools, he can show what he has retained.

We find it interesting that reading platforms for early school children include read-aloud options, but as students progress, these mechanisms are removed and often have to be applied using some sort of third-party tool. It is almost as though it is assumed that students grow out of using so-called "training wheels," whereas we argue that such supports should never be referred to as training wheels in the first place. Rather, it is a mechanism of assistive technology that provides an additional and alternative layer of support so that students can succeed in a course or with a specific piece of material.

Requiring students to print out something because you do annotations best in print form is no longer acceptable. You are putting some students at a disadvantage, and reading in a digital format versus hardcopy requires quite different skills and attention spans (Wolf, 2018). Now, by no means are we saying that you shouldn't share with your students how you engage with a text, how you take notes, analyze, and work toward comprehension. This, in fact, is a wonderful exercise to have them see what your process looks like in practice. Where this becomes problematic is when we stop there. Instead, consider sharing your processes and why they work for you, then ask them to reflect on what works for them. It is possible that they may not know what works, but again, this is where offering options that can work with assistive technology can be so impactful.

Next, consider **speech-to-text** technologies that come in a variety of forms, including Google Doc's Voice Typing function and AI assistants like Siri and Alexa on our smart devices. These afford users the ability to convert spoken language into written text. While this can be a safety feature that folks often employ when in a car – for example, sending a text message while driving – it originally was intended to give users with visual impairments the opportunity to compose in a computing space. Braille key functions can offer the same option in terms of computer composing, but speech-to-text, in particular, has become ubiquitous in such a way that many folks use it on a regular basis, whether a specific disability warrants it or not. Students, likewise, who may struggle to write a paper but say that they can talk out their ideas with ease can certainly take advantage of this option, making assistive technology a means of pushing through any number of barriers.

We acknowledge that this may be another bone of contention for some instructors who view writing and speaking as two separate skills, and we don't disagree, but modern technology allows users to compose in different ways on demand. Perhaps a way of narrowing the gap between writing and speaking skills is to think of composing in terms of communication, which ultimately brings many forms of expressing meaning into play. In this sense, the act of writing and speaking are almost synonymous, and rather than encouraging students only to do one or the other, they limit the possibilities afforded to them by engaging with different mechanisms of composition. Like many others, Cat regularly uses Siri to dictate text messages and notes while she's driving or walking. The ability to capture ideas and ways of expressing them on the spot empowers writers in ways that simply sitting in front of a notepad or computer might miss. It also supports the type of learner who must process information aloud before whittling down to the core of their ideas. In any case, options are key, and we strongly encourage you to discuss different speech-to-text options immediately available to students on the devices they use on a daily basis. Not only might you learn something new that may be helpful in your course design efforts, but you may help some students unlock tools that can make their school experience much more equitable.

Finally, let's discuss **image-to-text** technologies. The most common form is alternative text or alt text, so named because it offers users an alternative means of access to visual content. Alt text has become essential for users with limited visual ability and for those navigating documents through text-to-speech platforms. While alt text is a must in course design, it also serves as a metric for how teacher-designers think about communicating with visuals. Ashlyn, for example, loves to design with images, color, shape, and space – sometimes a bit too much. She often struggles to remove elements from a design partly because she believes they are inherently necessary to the composition. However, when Ashlyn began learning to use alt text, it offered an opportunity to consider: is this image/visual necessary to understand the activity/assignment, or is it purely decorative? Embellishments are not bad, but a composition with fifteen decorative elements to one visual that enhances one's understanding of the task points to a problem. A student using a screen reader to engage with a text with the 15 to 1 ratio may feel particularly marginalized. Why is so much decoration needed for the task? Does this somehow distract from the actual assignment? What am I missing by not being able to interpret images in the same way?

Accessibility checkers often mark images that haven't had an adequate alt text description, with some offering the option of "decoration" rather than a short explanation. Writing good alt text can be really tricky. As mentioned in the "Engagement" chapter, Cat and Ashlyn struggle on opposite ends of the spectrum of detail-laden compositions – Cat is strong with brevity and concision, and Ashlyn with expansive detail. Alt text requires one to err on the side of brief and context specific. Explain the "why" of the image – why does it matter, why does it support the learning goal, why is it part of the assignment, and so on. Concision becomes a unique challenge here to address all the "whys," appropriately, but a well-selected image that helps communicate meaning makes the process of writing alt text much easier.

Here are a couple of quick best practices in writing alt text:

- Consider how you would read this webpage aloud to someone who cannot access the page right now.
- Do you find yourself glossing over the images and not mentioning them because they don't add to the text? If so, what changes in images might be helpful that could support someone's understanding of the text?
- What is the most important information someone needs to know when engaging with an image? Once identified, start the alt text description with the priority one information first.
- Keep it short but context-specific. Ask yourself: what is the purpose of this image?, and then write a brief sentence description.
- For complex images like graphs, charts, data sets, and others, longer descriptions in a two-part form will be necessary. The first part of the description should follow the model of other image alt text – essentially, it is a one-sentence explanation of the image purpose (e.g., Pie chart of

course modality types at the university). The second part expands and describes the visual information (e.g., 55% asynchronous, 15% synchronous, 10% hybrid, and 20% in-person).

We also include closed captioning in this section since these often include descriptions of visual elements of videos to enhance understanding. In fact, Cat and Ashlyn both insist on having captions turned on when watching TV or videos, and we both miss the captions when we're in movie theaters. Perhaps many of you can relate to this practice, but in case you don't, Cat has trouble understanding plot points and detailed dialogue without being able to read them. She used to wonder why she struggled in this area with movies and TV series since her husband could easily follow and recall even the most complicated storylines. Captions have fundamentally changed how Cat experiences video formats and processes in-depth visual content.

Student Products and Assistive Technology

In addition to the best practices for creating course content already discussed, we encourage you to, whenever possible, explicitly teach students to follow basic accessibility guidelines in their work as well. For example, Cat spends a good deal of time teaching students how using built-in heading styles allows them to use the document outline functions in Google Docs and Microsoft Word and create hyperlinked tables of content. Cat incorporates these expectations into her assessment of student work to further emphasize the importance of these practices. Ashlyn likewise spends a lot of time modeling how students can use space, shape, color, and visuals to help support a text's meaning. Such moves open discussion for text emphasis and alt text as crucial accessibility elements that must be included in effective compositions. In short, both Cat and Ashlyn advocate for students to learn how to consider imagined and real audiences needs and preferences in a way that invites all in and works hard to combat issues of marginalization.

Limitations of Accessibility Checkers

It's important to step back for a moment and discuss the prevalence of using accessibility checkers that come in a variety of forms. These are tools that purport to evaluate digital content for compliance to accessibility standards, and they include the popular WAVE tool and built-in tools like Canvas's accessibility checker. We want to caution you not to become over reliant on such tools because we've found them to have serious limitations. In short, we advise adhering to the best practices outlined previously and then running a checker, rather than allowing such tools to guide you toward accessible content.

Here are just a few noted limitations that are commonly known:

Limited Scope: Accessibility checkers often focus on specific aspects of accessibility, such as alt text for images or heading structure. While they can catch some common issues, they may not cover all the complexities of accessibility or identify more nuanced barriers that individuals using screen reading tools may encounter.

Contextual Understanding: Accessibility checkers lack the ability to understand the context in which content is presented. For instance, they may not recognize if the alt text provided for an image is truly informative and meaningful for users who are using a screen reader.

False Positives and Negatives: Accessibility checkers may generate false positives (incorrectly identifying an element as inaccessible) or false negatives (failing to detect actual accessibility issues). This can lead to confusion and potentially cause content creators to make unnecessary changes or overlook genuine accessibility concerns.

Evaluation Limitations: The effectiveness of an accessibility checker depends on the accuracy and completeness of its evaluation rules. Some checkers might not keep pace with evolving accessibility standards and guidelines, leading to outdated recommendations.

Platform-Specific Variations: The accessibility of digital content can be affected by the platform on which it is viewed, such as web browsers, assistive technology, or devices. An accessibility checker might not account for these variations, resulting in inconsistent user experiences.

Lack of User Experience Perspective: Accessibility checkers primarily focus on technical compliance but may not consider the overall user experience. Your course site might meet all technical requirements but still be challenging to navigate or use effectively for your students who have different ways of navigating and consuming course content.

Non-Detectable Issues: Some accessibility barriers cannot be automatically detected by software. For instance, you always need to ensure that your language is clear and student-oriented, which requires human judgment and intervention.

Focus on Content, Not Interaction: Accessibility checkers often evaluate static content, like documents or images, but may not fully assess the accessibility of interactive elements or dynamic content, like videos or slideshows.

Model in Practice

Understanding the basics of these technologies is important for developing awareness about how to create content that allows students access to effectively using them. We recommend the following guidelines for instructional content (Figure 4.1).

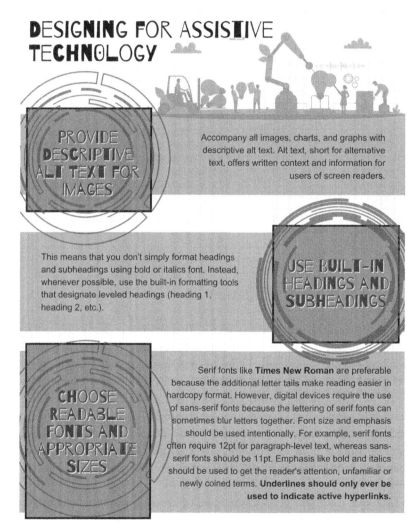

Figure 4.1 A quick reference guide for including various accessibility features that work with assistive technologies, such as alt text, leveled headings, font types/sizes, and so on (*Continued*)

Provide captions and/or transcripts when incorporating videos or audio. As mentioned earlier, some students need to hear content, while others need to view it. Offering captions and transcripts allows all students to engage with content in the best way for them on any given day.

INCLUDE CAPTIONS AND TRANSCRIPTS FOR MULTIMEDIA

OFFER MULTIPLE FORMATS FOR COURSE MATERIALS

Provide course materials in various formats, such as PDF, Word, or HTML, to give students flexibility in choosing formats that align with their assistive technology preferences. This doesn't always mean more work for you. For example, if you've used the guidelines above in your course site, students who need to can download it in PDF or HTML formats and use screen readers. Of course, you can also upload document forms of assignments and resources to be certain that you've met this goal.

Figure 4.1 (Continued)

Putting Your Layers Together

Like other areas of course design, considering assistive technologies and their ability to interpret your course content for users can seem overwhelming at first, but in reality, developing habits of mind toward accessibility in this way will greatly improve your own digital literacy skills. For example, when you create alt text, you are considering your own graphics through a different perspective, expanding your own understanding of what you intend for your students to take away from any given visual. Likewise, once you get in the habit of using built-in style headings, you'll appreciate the ability to use the document outline function with more intention and ease. These skills are as important for you as they are for your students.

Likewise, once you get into the habit of creating your content for accessibility, taking that extra step to generate accessible alternative formats will become quick and simple. Remember that the goal is to ensure that all students in your course, regardless of ability, can learn and succeed in your course. We imagine a day when students with a range of (dis)abilities can access learning as easily as anyone else without having the extra labor of documenting their disabilities and then requesting complicated accommodations.

Perhaps most importantly, practicing the sort of attentiveness to assistive technologies provides an opportunity for you to make this work visible to students. When they see us modeling practices that are integral to our pedagogy, they see us as lifelong learners as well. Such a rapport is crucial to any classroom because it helps us remember that learning isn't about checking boxes off but rather an ever-expanding experience of being human and moving through this world. Thus, the charge to take up accessibility work becomes a means of paying it forward: if we care about what it means to be human, we must invite students on that journey with us. They can learn practices they can carry into the world and teach us new ways of thinking about accessibility from the learner's perspective.

Checklist

- [ ] Use clear and concise language in all materials to enhance comprehension for all students, including those relying on assistive technologies.
- [ ] Accompany all images, charts, and graphs with descriptive alt text to provide context and information for visually impaired students using screen readers.
- [ ] Organize content with properly formatted headings and subheadings to enable efficient navigation for screen reader users.
- [ ] Choose readable fonts and appropriate font sizes to ensure legibility for all learners, including those with visual impairments.
- [ ] Include captions and transcripts for multimedia elements (videos or audio) to cater to students with hearing impairments or those who prefer reading the content.
- [ ] Offer course materials in multiple formats, such as PDF, Word, or HTML, to provide flexibility for students with diverse assistive technology preferences.

References and Resources

Akpan, P & Beard A. (2013). Overview of assistive technology possibilities for teachers to enhance academic outcomes of all students. *Universal Journal of Educational Research*, *1*(2), 113–118. https://doi.org/10.13189/ujer.2013.010211

Ahmad, F. K. (2015). Use of assistive technology in inclusive education: Making room for diverse learning needs. *Transcience*, *6*(2), 62–77.

Borgman, J., & Dockter, J. (2018). Considerations of access and design in the online writing classroom. *Computers and Composition*, 2018(4), 94–105.

Borgman, J., & McArdle, C. (Eds.). (2019). *Personal, accessible, responsive, strategic: Resources and strategies for online writing instructors.* Fort Collins, CO: WAC Clearinghouse.

Boyle, C., & Rivers, N. A. (2016). A version of access. *Technical Communication Quarterly, 25*(1),29–47. doi:10.1080/10572252.2016.1113702

Chambers, D. (2019, October 30). Assistive technology to enhance inclusive education. *Oxford Research Encyclopedia of Education.* Retrieved 29 Jan. 2024, from https://oxfordre.com/education/view/10.1093/acrefore/9780190264093.001.0001/acrefore-9780190264093-e-155

Desmond, D., Layton, N., Bentley, J., Boot, F. H., Borg, J., Dhungana, B. M., Gallagher, P., Gitlow, L., Gowran, R. J., Groce, N., Mavrou, K., Mackeogh, T., McDonald, R., Pettersson, C., & Scherer, M. J. (2018). Assistive technology and people: A position paper from the first global research, innovation and education on assistive technology (GREAT) summit. *Disability and Rehabilitation: Assistive Technology, 13*(5), 437–444. https://doi.org/10.1080/17483107.2018.1471169

Dolmage, J. T. (2014). "Mētis." In *Disability rhetoric.* Syracuse: Syracuse University Press, muse.jhu.edu/book/27790

Dolmage, J. T. (2017). *Academic ableism: Disability and higher education* (1st ed.). Ann Arbor, MI: University of Michigan Press. https://doi.org/10.3998/mpub.9708722

Educause.edu. (n.d.). Accessibility and accommodations. Retrieved from https://www.educause.edu/ecar/research-publications/student-technology-report-supporting-the-whole-student/2020/accessibility-and-accommodations

Fernández-Batanero, J. M., Montenegro-Rueda, M., Fernández-Cerero, J. & Garcia-Martinez, I. (2022). Assistive technology for the inclusion of students with disabilities: A systematic review. *Educational Technology Research and Development, 70,* 1911–1930. https://doi.org/10.1007/s11423-022-10127-7

Foley, A., & Ferri, B. A. (2012). Technology for people, not disabilities: Ensuring access and inclusion. *Journal of Research in Special Educational Needs, 12*(4), 192–200. Retrieved from https://onlinelibrary-wiley-com.librarylink.uncc.edu/doi/pdf/10.1111/j.1471-3802

Garland-Thomson, R. (1997). *Extraordinary bodies: Figuring physical disability in American culture and literature.* New York, NY: Columbia University Press.

Gronseth, S. L., & Dalton, E. M. (Eds.). (2020). *Universal access through inclusive instructional design: International perspectives on UDL.* London: Routledge.

Hitt, A. (2018). Foregrounding accessibility through (inclusive) universal design in professional communication curricula. *Business and Professional Communication Quarterly, 81*(1), 52–65. doi:10.1177/2329490617739884

Joyce, A. (2022). *Inclusive design.* USA: Nielsen Norman Group. Retrieved from https://www.nngroup.com/articles/inclusive-design/

Langdon, P., Lazar, J., Heylighen, A., & Dong, H. (Eds.). (2018). *Breaking down barriers usability, accessibility and inclusive design* (1st ed.). Berlin: Springer International Publishing. https://doi.org/10.1007/978-3-319-75028-6

Lyner-Cleophas, M. (2019). Assistive technology enables inclusion in higher education: The role of Higher and Further Education Disability Services Association. *African Journal of Disability, 8*(1), 1–6. https://doi.org/10.4102/ajod.v8i0.558

Mahaffey, C., & Walden, A. (2019). # teachingbydesign: Complicating accessibility in the tech-mediated classroom. In K. Becnel (Ed.), *Emerging technologies in virtual learning environments* (pp. 38–66). Hershey, PA: IGI Global.

McNicholl, A., Casey, H., Desmond, D., & Gallagher, P. (2021). The impact of assistive technology use for students with disabilities in higher education: a systematic review. *Disability and Rehabilitation: Assistive Technology, 16*(2), 130–143. https://doi.org/10.1080/17483107.2019.1642395

Oswal, S., & Meloncon, L. (2014). Paying attention to accessibility when designing online courses in technical and professional communication. *Journal of Business and Technical Communication, 28*(3), 271–300.

Persson, H., Åhman, H., Yngling, A. A., & Gulliksen, J. (2015). Universal design, inclusive design, accessible design, design for all: different concepts—One goal? On the concept of accessibility—Historical, methodological and philosophical aspects. *Universal Access in the Information Society, 14*(4), 505–526. https://doi.org/10.1007/s10209-014-0358-z

Walden, A. C. (2022). Necessity is the mother of invention: Accessibility pre, inter, & post pandemic. *Computers and Composition 66*, 102740. Accessed January 30, 2024. https://doi.org/10.1016/j.compcom.2022.102740

Wilson, J. C., & Lewiecki-Wilson, C. (2001). *Disability, rhetoric, and the body. Embodied rhetorics: Disability in language and culture* (pp. 1–27). Carbondale, IL: Southern Illinois University Press.

Wolf, M. (2018). *Reader, come home: The reading brain in a digital world* (1st ed.). New York, NY: Harper, an imprint of HarperCollinsPublishers.

Zitkus, E., Langdon, P., & Clarkson, P. J. (2013). Inclusive design advisor: Understanding the design practice before developing inclusivity tools. *Journal of Usability Studies, 8*(4), 127–143.

Online Privacy   5

Introduction/Overview

It might be surprising that we devote a whole chapter to online privacy, something that may seem a bit removed from discussions of course design, but the increasing role of technology in the classroom brings with it a myriad of concerns that are too-often overlooked. This chapter explores the various policies in higher education that intersect with online privacy with an eye toward protecting student and instructor privacy.

Many of you are at least somewhat aware of the existence of data brokers and digital profiles. Some of you may even practice what's referred to as DIY privacy by using secure browsers or VPNs, turning off location tracking on your cell phone, and some of you may have resisted creating social media accounts or purchasing things online because you want to avoid this type of surveillance and tracking. Sadly, these DIY practices only make a small dent in the data collected, sold, and manipulated into digital profiles, and those digital profiles are purchased by companies that use algorithms to sort users into racial, economic, and gender categories that may or may not reflect users accurately or fairly.

What Is Online Privacy?

Scholars define *online privacy* as a user's "freedom from intrusion or scrutiny" (Igo, 2018, p. 4), and an individual right to "liberty, freedom, individual dignity, and the right to be let alone" (Mills, 2015, p. 12). For our purposes, online privacy refers to the ability to control one's digital footprint and avoid undue surveillance and tracking in online and digital spaces. Much like the rest of society, students consistently express concerns about their online privacy, while at the same time they share personal information, their own

DOI: 10.4324/9781003485476-6

and others, when interacting in online spaces (Nissenbaum, 2010; Brooks, 2016; Fleming & Adkins, 2016; Lin, 2017; Weinberger et al., 2017; Dogruel & Jöckel, 2019). This disconnect between sentiment and behavior offers scholars a lot of fodder, but the takeaway is that it's incumbent on instructors to have a basic understanding of algorithmic surveillance and how it might impact digital learning environments.

Teacher-scholars who focus on student privacy agree that, from an instructional standpoint, the more information students have about how algorithms work and the risks inherent in them, the more empowered students will be when considering which apps and web tools they choose to share personal information with (Scheid, 2019; Park & Vance, 2021; Marín et al., 2023). This understanding of algorithmic data collection, manipulation, and sharing could be especially useful for students who need a foundation for protecting their own data, outside and inside the classroom, and for advocating against such widespread corporate practices.

Online Privacy and Accessibility

Defining accessibility through the lens of online privacy may seem counterintuitive, but when it comes down to an individual student-user's privacy, the apps and web tools an instructor uses to distribute course content or requires for student participation can complicate accessibility for students attuned to privacy issues. For example, if a student actively protects their digital profile through incognito tools or limited online accounts, asking them to create an active and identifiable account outside a protected domain (and sometimes even within protected domains) presents a very real access issue. They must choose between full participation in a course and adhering to their own personal standards of privacy.

Of critical concern are platforms that require students to share their work publicly on the web. One primary example is something like a class portfolio website. Much of the impetus toward having students do such open work stems from the need for real-world skills in multimodal and digital design. We don't propose that this good work should cease. Instead, we aim to merge scholarship about online privacy and digital literacy. Just like efforts to overcome racism, sexism, classism, and all the other societal injustices, we believe that educators play a critical role in the effort to shift public apathy toward demanding higher ethical standards for user data and online privacy. In fact, privacy is the newest front for such social justice work (Taylor, 2017; AAEEBL, n.d.; DRPC, n.d.).

How does this relate to accessibility? Because if we say we want to resist anti-racist systems, then online privacy should become part of that conversation. In short, current online privacy practices perpetuate inequities. Even if you think, "Well, my students aren't doing anything in my classroom that could harm their digital profile. What's the big deal if a student posts their thoughts or links to their writing on Padlet?" Consider that security in sharing personal thoughts and writing on the web is borne from privilege. For underserved populations, expressed ideas about beliefs and values can be used to determine whether someone is worthy of employment, housing, and/or credit (Gilman & Green, 2018; Lai & Tanner, 2022; Lee & Chin, 2022). This is called *digital redlining*, and it hurts vulnerable populations disproportionately (Lambright, 2019).

Methods and Application

Evaluating online privacy in your classroom goes hand in hand with two other chapters we recommend you consult alongside this one: "Choosing Technologies" and "Understanding Assistive Technologies." The intention is not to overcomplicate the process, but rather to demonstrate the intersections between why and when to consider the various insights from the three chapters' discussions of classroom technology. Let's begin by looking at the major privacy regulations governing educational realms, and then consider how those regulations apply to a sample, generic classroom technology. For clarity, we have chosen not to discuss an existing app or web tool to avoid disparaging or promoting any certain one.

Major Privacy Regulations

Regulating users' online privacy is a murky endeavor. Part of the issue is that lawmakers lack understanding of the breadth and purpose of data collection. As we write this chapter, the dangers and possibilities of artificial intelligence (AI) technologies are being hotly debated. For this reason, we anticipate new regulations to enter the law books, but for now, there are only a few basic, limited laws that impact classroom technology and online privacy.

FERPA: or the Family Educational Rights and Privacy Act, is the overarching US federal regulation for educational privacy. It protects the educational records of students of all ages, beginning at kindergarten and spanning through postsecondary levels. FERPA applies to schools that receive federal funds, which includes things like Pell grants and federal student loans, so the vast majority of both public and private schools must adhere to FERPA regulations. Note that FERPA protections are limited to educational records, things like grades, class schedules, attendance records, and so on (FERPA, 2021).

COPPA: or the Children's Online Privacy Protection Act, passed in 2000, is one of the most significant US federal regulations. It prohibits online data collection and sharing for children under age thirteen. While it originally only applied to websites designed and marketed to children, a 2013 update expanded its regulation to limit data collection if a website or app operator becomes aware that a user is under thirteen. COPPA requires that online entities post their privacy policy and get parental consent to collect underage users' data and allow parents to request their child's data for deletion (Federal Trade Commission [FTC], 2002).

GDPR: or the General Data Protection Regulation, is perhaps the world's most comprehensive online privacy regulation. Even though it only technically applies to nations in the European Union, most institutions strive to adhere to GDPR guidelines, especially if they have large populations of international transfer students. Passed in May 2018, the GDPR bans the collection of certain categories of personal data:

- a name and surname;
- a home address;
- an email address such as name.surname@company.com;
- an identification card number;
- location data (for example the location data function on a mobile phone)*;
- an Internet Protocol (IP) address;
- a cookie ID*;
- the advertising identifier of your phone;
- data held by a hospital or doctor, which could be a symbol that uniquely identifies a person (European Commission, n.d.).

CCPA: the California Consumer Privacy Act is a state statute intended to enhance privacy rights and consumer protection for residents of California, United States. It grants consumers the right to know what personal information is being collected about them and the right to access that information, among other provisions. The CCPA also imposes regulations on the sale of personal information and requires businesses to provide a clear and conspicuous link on their website's homepage titled "Do Not Sell My Personal Information" to enable consumers to opt out of the sale of their personal information (CCPA, 2023).

Evaluating Privacy Policies

To evaluate the privacy standards of any given technology means engaging with privacy policies, which is a daunting task for most users. Research shows that most privacy policies are written at levels beyond the capability of most users, and it seems this is intentional (Jensen & Potts, 2004; Steinfeld, 2016). In fact, developers and companies wrap their privacy policies in legalese that protects them from being sued by users who may inadvertently discover their personal information has been sold or shared with third parties (Klosowski, 2023). Regardless of purpose, companies craft their policies in vastly different ways. The design and language choices prevent readers from making informed decisions as to whether they want to allow companies access to their information and the repercussions of granting such access (Furnell & Phippen, 2012). Additionally, research suggests that privacy policies are often long, difficult to read (Sumeeth et al., 2010), and purposely crafted to prevent readers from understanding what data is collected and how that data is used (Markel, 2005; Lindh & Nolin, 2016).

The good news is that as awareness and concern have increased around this issue so too have the resources. Through practice and habit, instructors *can* become proficient in quickly scanning privacy policies or using tools that do the work of evaluating online privacy settings. In this section, we offer several ways to navigate the privacy policy of a technology.

Using a privacy checker. Perhaps the quickest and simplest way to evaluate a technology's privacy is through a privacy checking website or app, which offers comprehensive information about online privacy and includes expert evaluations of most popular apps. Through these watchdog sites, you can find evaluations of apps and web tools across all educational levels, as well as those used in professional and private settings.

Scanning for terms and phrases. If you can't find an expert evaluation of a privacy policy, you can go directly to the policy and scan for key concerns related to collecting, sharing, and storing personal data. Nearly all apps and web tools collect data, and many of them store data long term. Collecting and storing information isn't necessarily a bad thing since it's user-friendly for your pharmacy app to store your prescription details or even for your social media app to store your preferences to generate content that you enjoy most. The problem is not the collection, storing, or even the algorithmic sorting of your personal information. At issue is the selling and/or sharing of your personal information, preferences, and habits to third parties for profit.

Model in Practice

Navigating the legalese of privacy policies may seem impossible, but in the Figure 5.1 are some terms and phrases you can scan for when evaluating privacy settings. Another quick tip is to consider using key commands to "find" these terms throughout the policies so that you can quickly locate what you need.

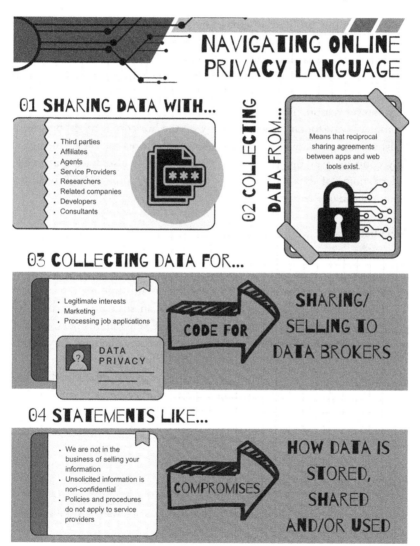

Figure 5.1 An overview of common terms and phrases that are included in online privacy statements in addition to what the language actually means in practice

Putting Your Layers Together

Online privacy is another one of those aspects of modern teaching that can seem daunting to deal with. We hope after reading this chapter you now see that privacy is both important and attainable. As instructors, we are responsible for not only protecting our students but also for guiding them toward questioning when and where their personal data is being collected and/or sold for corporate profit or even more nefarious purposes.

We want to reiterate one final time that an accessible course is one that allows every student to participate. Don't let the prevalent nature of sharing personal information via social media and digital streaming lead you to disregard the privacy of students who want to protect their digital footprint, for whatever reason. This topic is a dynamic one. New legislation and public emphasis on student privacy is likely on the horizon. It might be wise to incorporate some way of gauging student preferences each year through an early course survey or discussion forum. If nothing else, having a broader understanding of data collection and online privacy policies will mean that you are ahead of the game.

Checklist

☐ Are the privacy policies clearly accessible? Do they have coded language that suggests they sell/share personal data to data brokers?

☐ Is the privacy policy language accessible to all students, regardless of reading ability and/or native language? Can students determine for themselves whether or not the technology sells/shares personal data to data brokers? What repercussions will students incur if they choose to protect their privacy and not use the technology?

☐ Compare how the technology functions against established privacy norms. Is the activity something that should become a permanent part of a student's digital footprint?

References and Resources

Association for Authentic, Experiential & Evidence-Based Learning. (AAEEBL). (n.d.). *Aaeebl.org*. Retrieved from https://aaeebl.org

Brooks, D. C. (2016). ECAR study of undergraduate students and information technology, *EDUCAUSE*, p. 22; https://er.educause.edu/-/media/files/library/2016/10/ers1605.pdf?la=en&hash=AC14113E8D1DDD26AEB39856981C1F331D0A249F

California Privacy Protection Act (CCPA). (2023). Retrieved from https://oag.ca.gov/privacy/ccpa

Common Sense Media. (2021, September 1). *Privacy evaluation for discord – Talk, chat & hangout.* Commonsense.org. https://privacy.commonsense.org/evaluation/Discord---Talk-Chat--Hangout

Digital Privacy Rhetorical Collective (DRPC). (n.d.). *Drpcollective.com.* Retrieved from https://drpcollective.com

Dogruel, L., & Jöckel, S. (2019). Risk perception and privacy regulation preferences from a cross-cultural perspective: A qualitative study among German and U.S. smartphone users. *International Journal of Communication, 13*, 1764–1783.

European Commission. (n.d.) What is personal data? Retrieved from https://commission.europa.eu/law/law-topic/data-protection/reform/what-personal-data_en

Federal Education and Privacy Act (FERPA). (2021). Retrieved from https://www2.ed.gov/policy/gen/guid/fpco/ferpa/index.html

Federal Trade Commission. (2002, April). COPPA: Children's Online Privacy Protection Act. Federal Trade Commission. https://www.ftc.gov/sites/default/files/documents/rules/children%E2%80%99s-online-privacy-protection-rule-coppa/coppasurvey.pdf

Fleming, J. H., & Adkins, A. (2016, June 9). *Data Security: Not a Big Concern for Millennials,* Gallup, https://news.gallup.com/businessjournal/192401/data-security-not-big-concern-millennials.aspx

Furnell, S., & Phippen, A. (2012). Online privacy: a matter of policy? *Computer Fraud & Security, 2012*(8), 12–18. https://doi.org/10.1016/S1361-3723(12)70083-0

Gilman, M., & Green, R. (2018). The surveillance gap: The harms of extreme privacy and data marginalization. *New York University Review of Law and Social Change, 42*(2), 253.

Igo, S. E. (2018). *The known citizen: A history of privacy in modern America.* Cambridge, MA: Harvard UP.

Jensen, C., & Potts, C. (2004). Privacy policies as decision-making tools: An evaluation of online privacy notices. In *Proceedings of the SIGCHI Conference on Human Factors in Computing Systems* (Vol. 6, 1st ed., pp. 471–478). Retrieved from http://portal.acm.org/citation.cfm?id=985752

Klosowski, T. (2023). Here's what you're actually agreeing to when you accept a privacy policy. New York Times Wirecutter. Retrieved May 16, 2024, from https://www.nytimes.com/wirecutter/blog/what-are-privacy-policies/

Lai, S., & Tanner, B. (2022). Examining the intersection of data privacy and civil rights. In *TechTank [BLOG].* The Brookings Institution.

Lambright, K. (2019). Digital redlining: The Nextdoor App and the neighborhood of make-believe. *Cultural Critique, 103*(1), 84–90. https://doi.org/10.1353/cul.2019.0023

Lee, N. T., & Chin, C. (2022). *Police surveillance and facial recognition: Why data privacy is imperative for communities of color.* The Brookings Institution. Retrieved from Social Science Premium Collection https://www.proquest.com/reports/police-surveillance-facial-recognition-why-data/docview/2659132681/se-2

Lin, Y. (2017, February 1). A reflective commentary of teaching critical thinking of privacy and surveillance in UK higher education. *Big Data & Society.* https://journals.sagepub.com/doi/full/10.1177/2053951717694054

Lindh, M., & Nolin, J. (2016). Information We Collect: Surveillance and Privacy in the Implementation of Google Apps for Education. *European Educational Research Journal, 15*, 644–663. https://doi.org/10.1177/1474904116654917

Markel, M. (2005). The rhetoric of misdirection in corporate privacy-policy statements. *Technical Communical Quarterly*, *14*(2). 197–214. https://www.tandfonline.com/doi/abs/10.1207/s15427625tcq1402_5

Marín, V. I., Carpenter, J. P., Tur, G., & Williamson-Leadley, S. (2023). Social media and data privacy in education: An international comparative study of perceptions among pre-service teachers. *Journal of Computers in Education (the Official Journal of the Global Chinese Society for Computers in Education)*, *10*(4), 769–795. https://doi.org/10.1007/s40692-022-00243-x

Mills, J. L. (2015). *Privacy in the New Media Age*. Gainesville, FL: Florida UP.

Nissenbaum, H. (2010). *Privacy in context: Technology, policy, and the integrity of social life*. Stanford: Stanford UP.

Park, J. & Vance, A. (2021). Data privacy in higher education: Yes students care. *Educause*. Retrieved from https://er.educause.edu/articles/2021/2/data-privacy-in-higher-education-yes-students-care

Scheid, M. (2019). The educator's role: Privacy, confidentiality, and security in the classroom. *Studentprivacycompass.org*. Retrieved from https://studentprivacycompass.org/scheid1/

Steinfeld, N. (2016). "I agree to the terms and conditions": (How) do users read privacy policies online? An eye-tracking experiment. *Computers in Human Behavior*, *55*, 992–1000. https://doi.org/10.1016/j.chb.2015.09.038

Sumeeth, M., Singh, R. I., & Miller, J. (2010, January–March). Are online privacy policies readable? *International Journal of Information Security and Privacy*, *4*(1), 93–2116. https://www.igi-global.com/gateway/article/43058

Taylor, L. (2017). What is data justice? The case for connecting digital rights and freedoms globally. *Big Data & Society*, *4*(2), 205395171773633–14. https://doi.org/10.1177/2053951717736335

Weinberger, M., Zhitomirsky-Geffet, M., & Bouhnik, D. (2017). Factors affecting users' online privacy literacy among students in Israel. *Online Information Review*, *41*(5), 655–671. Retrieved from http://search.proquest.com.ezproxy.libproxy.db.erau.edu/docview/1935190728?accountid=27203

Choosing Classroom Technologies

6

Overview/Introduction

As longtime college instructors, we witnessed the complete transformation of higher education and its relationship with technology. When we were undergraduate students, learning management systems had not entered the scene yet. We received hard copies of the syllabus and all assignment descriptions. We took copious handwritten notes so that we could pass handwritten essay exams and penciled-in scantron tests. Once we became instructors, our institution first adopted Blackboard, and then Moodle, and then Canvas, and with each new LMS, we had to re-learn how to design our classes.

Alongside the shift toward learning management systems came the notion of technology as a tool for engagement. Teachers shifted from using overhead projectors to creating PowerPoint presentations, and then moved onto flashier online presentation tools like Prezi. Next came online flash card creators and fun quizzing tools, and as we write this chapter, virtual teaching assistants are emerging like ChatGPT and other AIs. Our point here is that once technology entered the classroom, its adoption and usage became an embedded part of teaching and continues to be arguably the single most important tool for learning in modern times (Warschauer & Matuchniak, 2010; US DOE, 2017; Selwyn, 2020).

This chapter aims to put technology in its rightful place in the classroom, as a tool that can be harnessed rather than a panacea for teaching. We hope you'll come away from this discussion with a sense of empowerment and importance for your role as a teacher. We reject the assertion that technology itself can teach students at anywhere near the level of an expert human. The decisions you make regarding how and when or which technologies to use in

DOI: 10.4324/9781003485476-7

your classroom can have great benefits, no doubt, but they can also produce overrated and underwhelming experiences for students who live in a taxing world of endless exposure to flashy screens and whizbang tools.

What Constitutes Classroom Technology?

For the purposes of this chapter, we will limit our discussion to apps and tools that you have some say in adopting. This means we've chosen not to address learning management systems that are typically outside an instructor's decision-making authority. Thus, classroom technology refers to the various tools and resources used to enhance teaching and learning. These can include multimedia tools like videos, infographics, and audio files. They might include new and emerging technologies like chatbots, online quizzes, or games. They might also include annotation tools that students can use to read and research, or feedback tools that teachers or classmates can use to promote interactivity and reflection or revision. Notice that we're avoiding naming any specific tools or tech, an intentional move on our part because of their ephemeral nature. Instead, we hope to foster a practice of continuous reflection on the effectiveness of the tools you have used, as well as a hearty evaluation of any new tech you consider adding.

Accessibility and Classroom Technologies

Classroom technologies present the most complicated aspect of accessibility since any one app or tool can both enhance and hinder student learning, depending on their preferences, digital literacy skills, and learning differences. For example, if your pedagogical goal is to level the playing field for socioeconomically disadvantaged students who may have fewer developed technology skills, then you'll lean toward technologies that are more intuitive and quicker to learn, but this decision may mean that more advanced students will be less challenged and feel shortchanged.

Another way to view this is to acknowledge that technology has become an embedded skill in virtually every professional role, so in many ways, exposure to and proficiency in more advanced technologies is part of the necessary learning for modern graduates (Warschauer & Matuchniak, 2010; McKinsey & Company, 2022). With this in mind, one approach might be to put off adopting more advanced technologies until students are in higher level classes. Another valid approach might be to choose fewer technologies and incorporate them more fully into various aspects of the course rather than choosing multiple, perhaps more simple, apps and tools.

Another important component related to accessibility relates to the prevalence in subscription levels. If you choose a technology because it offers free basic access, thinking that this allows students with fewer means to participate, you may inadvertently put those students at further disadvantage since their classmates can afford to pay for upgraded accounts that offer them more streamlined access or more features (Warschauer & Matuchniak, 2010; US DOE, 2017).

Finally, we encourage you to consult the chapter on Online Privacy as you make decisions about technologies to adopt for your classroom.

Methods and Application

In general, we recommend defaulting to university-supported technologies. This promotes both accessibility and privacy for students. Sometimes we inflate popular apps and websites with enhanced student engagement, but this isn't necessarily the case (see "Student Engagement" chapter for more information). For example, we teach at a school that uses Google Drive, which means that students and faculty have full access to the Google Suite and have on-campus technical support for all Google apps and tools within the university domain. As one example of how this impacts our decisions, for assignments that ask students to create visuals, we lean toward using Google Drawings rather than Canva or some other digital design platform tool because access and support are standard for all students.

Of course, we're aware of the very real differences in support offered from institution to institution, and we don't want to undermine the need for alternative classroom apps and tools. It's reasonable and appropriate to incorporate technologies not supported by the university, and this is where we hope to provide insights and guidance to help you think through when and where to incorporate a third-party technology into your classroom.

First, think about **why** you need a third-party technology. What will the tool or app help you or your students do? Does it allow students to practice a necessary skill? Does it allow them to manipulate or adapt an object or concept in order to expand their understanding? Your decision to add a third-party technology should be grounded in a pedagogical need rather than an attempt to simply add flash and flair to your lectures. You might also want to consider the number of technologies you're incorporating into your classroom. And the final **why** question might be to consider what critical skills students gain by using the technology. Is there a transferable, tactical skill or ability gained from adding this technology to your students' experience? For example, technologies that are merely teaching tools that add flash and fun won't necessarily be useful for students who aren't moving toward a teaching degree. However, most students would benefit from exposure to AI and practice in crafting prompts.

If you feel you do have a viable need for a third-party technology, then it's time to think about **which tool** is best. There are often multiple tools that do basically the same thing but with different access thresholds to consider. We discuss this in more depth in the "Online Privacy" chapter, but one big consideration is the privacy policy of the technology. Do they track students? Do they sell user data to data brokers? Some students are aware of online privacy and actively strive to limit their digital footprint, while others blindly create accounts with apps and tools that track and target them in unhealthy ways. You, as the instructor, have all the power and responsibility to ensure the safety and well-being of your students. For example, consider how students' beliefs and opinions evolve over their time in college. And also consider that prospective employers often search online to see what kind of digital presence a job candidate has. If you've assigned an activity that asks students to create an infographic or webpage that incorporates their personal narratives or value statements on a controversial topic, or if you ask them to create something for practice that isn't high quality, how might that digital footprint impact how they are perceived by future colleagues or supervisors?

As mentioned earlier, another critical thing to consider is whether the technology offers subscription levels. There is no way to realistically limit students to using basic free versions, and while *free* sounds like it equates to *accessible*, it's anything but. Your students with more economic resources may have very real advantages through paid access to higher subscription levels that offer more features, resulting in higher quality products, less labor, and even more privacy and protection.

Finally, when choosing third-party technologies, we encourage robust consideration about accessibility. Do you have students of varying digital literacy levels? How difficult is the tool to learn, teach, or use? If you have to spend an inordinate amount of time teaching students how to use a technology, or troubleshooting issues yourself, then perhaps that tool isn't a good fit. Likewise, some instructors forget that today's students use mobile devices more and more for coursework every year, and when they encounter barriers with technologies, they skip assignments or put them off until the last minute.

Overall, we recommend taking a birds-eye view of your course and evaluating your own goals and values: Do the benefits of adopting a third-party technology outweigh the risks?

Model in Practice

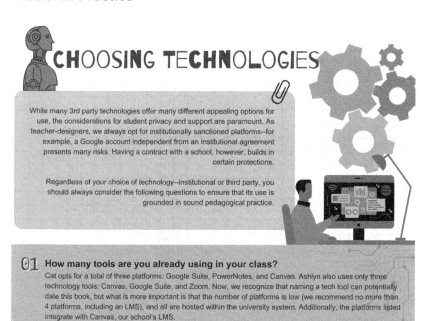

CHOOSING TECHNOLOGIES

While many 3rd party technologies offer many different appealing options for use, the considerations for student privacy and support are paramount. As teacher-designers, we always opt for institutionally sanctioned platforms—for example, a Google account independent from an institutional agreement presents many risks. Having a contract with a school, however, builds in certain protections.

Regardless of your choice of technology—institutional or third party, you should always consider the following questions to ensure that its use is grounded in sound pedagogical practice.

01 How many tools are you already using in your class?

Cat opts for a total of three platforms: Google Suite, PowerNotes, and Canvas. Ashlyn also uses only three technology tools: Canvas, Google Suite, and Zoom. Now, we recognize that naming a tech tool can potentially date this book, but what is more important is that the number of platforms is low (we recommend no more than 4 platforms, including an LMS, and all are hosted within the university system. Additionally, the platforms listed integrate with Canvas, our school's LMS.

02 What does this platform help you do? What does the platform help students do?

Cat opts to use Google Drawings as a blank slate to teach students basic digital design skills. The key here is that the drawing platform in the Google Suite isn't template-based; instead, students must apply the concepts of design, accessibility, and usability in creating a visual themselves. Ashlyn, on the other hand, uses Google Slides to teach students how platforms can be repurposed for other goals (e.g., making a digital document out of slides as opposed to using it only as a presentation tool.)

03 Why are you choosing this tool? Are you choosing it because it helps fulfill a pedagogical need that cannot be accomplished by other similar methods already used in a native tool?

In question 2, both Cat and Ashlyn discuss using Google platforms for various purposes in their classes. Now, a third-party site that has templates, or even native programs like Google Slides, has options where students do relatively little design work. However, in both cases, we choose to have students start from a blank space to build up designs from the beginning, thus learning the practice of design and gaining a better understanding of how to choose or build effective templates in the future.

Figure 6.1 An annotated explanation and examples of the choosing technologies heuristic   *(Continued)*

04 Does using/learning this tool contribute to students' transferable knowledge about digital composing/creating in the future work/production environment?

At least for now, Google is a widely used platform beyond the school environment. That said, it is inevitable that some other technology will replace the Google Suite at some point. However, cloud computing will be a mainstay; thus, having students learn to design and collaborate in these spaces is a must. Learning to design from scratch increases transferability. Students focus less on choosing/augmenting a template and instead practice methods of accessible design, which can then be imported into any platform.

05 Does this platform require you or students to create accounts?

Since all the platforms Cat and Ashlyn use are part of an institutional agreement, sign-ups are unnecessary. Instead, these are connected directly to student login information. In the past, when we asked students to sign up for accounts such as for web-building, we would choose sites that were free to use. The truth is that nothing is ever free, and often these accounts are riddled with privacy issues. In short, if accounts are required, take time to do a robust search of the user and privacy agreements, and be sure to spend extra time in our *Online Privacy* chapter.

06 Compare how the tech functions against established privacy norms. Is the activity something that should become a permanent part of a student's digital footprint?

As with question 5, creating accounts means establishing some sort of digital footprint. Though footprints are inevitable even within institutional memberships, the privacy expectations and data mining are vastly different and are often anonymized, scrubbed, and not sold for profit to third-party sites.

07 Does the platform have both free and paid options for use? What are the differences in these two options--potential affordances and constraints?

Higher education comes at a big price tag on a number of levels, and this is where allowing students to use programs already provided for within the system is ideal. In short, their student fees have already been paid for their use. Both Cat and Ashlyn avoid using programs that require an additional cost, and though students may ask to use other programs for various assignments, we take time to explain some of the risks and benefits of engaging with technology in this way.

08 How difficult is the tool to learn, teach, or use?

No doubt, any tech tool comes with its share of problems. Google programs, for example, can be unwieldy at times when students need to share documents. Yet, because both Cat and Ashlyn use these platforms on a regular basis, they are able to help or direct students to resources to help make adjustments with the tool. Another great advantage to us preaching the word on choosing institutional platforms? IT departments and helplines are standing by for students, meaning the ones to help them troubleshoot is not always on us as the instructors.

Figure 6.1 (Continued)

09 **Are there accessibility issues, such as lack of usable interface for mobile technology?**

Cat and Ashlyn prefer working on computers and designing the course content to function well on the computer. That said, students often have a very different approach, with many relying on mobile versions of the composing spaces we use. As such, we take time to play around with Google Suite, Canvas, and any other tech tool we use to ensure the content students engage with works on a mobile platform.

10 **Evaluate your own goals and values: Do the benefits of adopting the tech outweigh the risks?**

A close second to the pedagogical value of a technological tool, this question is key for both Cat and Ashlyn. Risk, most often, can be couched in terms of student privacy, which can be used to create digital footprints about students that may put them at risk. Issues of race, class, gender, sexual orientation, ability, ethnicity, culture, religious or political beliefs can easily be collected via site cookies on online "free" platforms. We go in-depth on these issues in the **Online Privacy** chapter, which we strongly encourage you to explore alongside this chapter as a companion piece.

Figure 6.1 (Continued)

Putting Your Layers Together

Overall, choosing technologies for teaching is not as straightforward as some seem to believe. The need for balance between engagement and accessibility cannot be overstated. We encourage you to resist the narrative that any technology platform can replace your critical role as the instructor. One thing we both do when a new technology becomes popular is to practice and play with the tool to see if it has transferable uses for our own work or personal lives. We approach the adoption of new apps and web tools as an ongoing process. One primary example is Cat's recent work with various AI tools to see which ones might be most helpful for her and thus her students. After determining that AI may have a role in her classroom, Cat then researched various AI apps to see which ones offer the most accessible and useful features for students. Then the next step in the process was to pilot an AI for a semester, where Cat surveyed her students and did some critical analysis of how that tool was (or was not) enhancing student learning and success. In the end, she decided to stick with the tool for a second semester so she could implement changes based on what she saw in the previous semester's pilot.

In short, we don't aim to create a sense of hesitancy or discourage the use of technology in teaching. Rather, the goal is to offer some basic minimum standards to empower instructors in selecting technologies that are accessible, relevant, and transferable. Technology is part of every aspect of our lives, including teaching and learning, but not every new bell or whistle will increase student engagement, and not every new digital tool is appropriate for every student.

Checklist

☐ Consider varying digital literacy skills and learning preferences of students when choosing technologies to incorporate into your classroom.

☐ When applicable, default to university-supported technologies for maximum accessibility and privacy.

☐ When incorporating third-party technologies, consider both your pedagogical needs and your students' long term transferable skill set.

☐ Evaluate the benefits of adopting any new technology against the associated risks.

References and Resources

McKinsey & Company. (2022). How technology is shaping learning in higher education. https://www.mckinsey.com/industries/education/our-insights/how-technology-is-shaping-learning-in-higher-education

Selwyn, N. (2020). Understanding the role of digital technologies in education: A review. *ScienceDirect*, *173*, 1–12. https://www.sciencedirect.com/science/article/pii/S0360131520303077

U.S. Department of Education. (2017). Reimagining the role of technology in higher education. https://tech.ed.gov/files/2017/01/Higher-Ed-NETP.pdf

Warschauer, M., & Matuchniak, T. (2010). New technology and digital worlds: Analyzing evidence of equity in access, use, and outcomes. *Review of Research in Education*, *34*(1), 179–225. https://journals.sagepub.com/doi/abs/10.3102/0091732X09349791

Course Mapping

7

Introduction/Overview

Contending with the content of a course in and of itself is a challenge but when you break it down into manageable steps under a clear process, it becomes easier. In this chapter, we will discuss strategies for visualizing a new or existing course through a series of mapping techniques. Mapping your course is an iterative process, meaning that you can create it at any stage of the design process and use it as a tool for evaluating and/or revising the course during or after the course is taught. Some faculty start their course design by creating a course map, while others build the course in their digital course site and then map it afterwards. The important thing to remember is that mapping techniques offer views of your course that are difficult to see otherwise. For example, say you have a large-scale end-of-course multimodal project. Accessibility, as we are concerned with in this text, requires us to envision how to best support student learning, scaffolding toward an end goal. This can certainly look different across courses, but course mapping allows us to see what support students need along the way to most effectively complete the final project. Questions you might consider are things like:

- What sort of technical skill sets do students need?
- Are these skill sets something that students would already have from previous, transferable knowledge?
- What sort of practice skills can I build in that are lower stakes?
- How might I involve students in the process of sharing with me what they need?

Without mapping, this scenario can become daunting for both students and instructors as it does not give us time to pause to consider what the real

DOI: 10.4324/9781003485476-8

outcomes are that we want students to gain in a timely, well-paced, and supported fashion.

What Is Course Mapping?

This is a good time to discuss the concept of modalities. We intend this manual to serve any tech-mediated course, including any course delivered through a learning management system (LMS), whether they are taught onsite or online, synchronous or asynchronous, or a hybrid approach which may have both in-person online students or in-person and online components to the course. And really, from the standpoint of accessibility, our course deliveries require us to have equitable, intuitive, and flexible access to course content materials regardless of modality. Gone are the days of classroom-restricted lectures that rely on students to take all their notes in part because such methods can quickly leave behind many potentially bright students that have diverse experiences that ultimately enrich our classrooms.

In a nutshell, a course map is a visual overview of your course, a bird's eye view of your calendar and course goals. Course maps come in different varieties and forms. Some instructors use this technique to align learning objectives (Wiggins & McTighe, 2005; Hartley & Cha, n.d.), while others find course maps helpful as a visual tool for designing or redesigning (remapping) an existing course (Stearns CTL, 2023; Hartley & Cha, n.d.). For our purposes, this part of the course-design process is more about the latter approach. We use course mapping as a way to practice *backward design*, which focuses on building a course based on learning goals rather than a textbook or assignment sequence (Jensen et al., 2017; Rhoads & Rocha-Hidalgo, 2020; Seok Nam, 2020). For a new course, this approach can be more difficult, so some instructors might find this step too tough as a starting point. If you find yourself unable to find a way into mapping a new course, we recommend that you try this technique on an existing course and see if it offers you a new perspective.

Course Mapping and Accessibility

It might not be evident at first glance how course mapping relates to accessibility, but there are several connections. First, the act of creating a course map affords space to zoom out and assess things like student workload and gaps in scaffolding. Second, course mapping also helps you structure your own workload, including building in time for feedback, grading, and even managing late submissions, an increasingly common concern post-COVID. Finally, and perhaps most importantly, course maps promote cohesion and alignment in a course. Let's expand on how each of these points connects to accessibility.

Zooming Out: Mapping can reveal spaces where students might need more support or instruction on a given concept, and if you find students continually performing poorly on a particular assignment, the course map might help you see gaps in scaffolding or opportunities to bolster learning. Let's return to the example mentioned in the introduction. You have found that the multimodal project, while successful in some ways, still presents issues in terms of accurately representing student learning. In this multimodal assignment, students are asked to create a visual representation of their growth in the course using a balanced combination of text and images. You notice that while the written reflection and assessments are strong, students are lacking in terms of good design choices. Rather than scrapping or modifying the end project, you might consider building in opportunities to discuss what good design practices look like, refer to resources such as universal design, and invite students to think of their text as a method for communicating with audiences that have a range of skill sets and needs. In this case, the scaffolded learning not only becomes about helping students improve on their capstone project, but it also sets them up for transferable skills attuned to accessibility issues. In short, the scaffolding and the project become about paying forward the work you yourself do when designing a course to accessibility.

Managing Workload: While instructors generally embed planning and prep time for class activities and assignments, they often underestimate or outright neglect to budget time for feedback and grading. Have you found yourself regretting when you assign major assignments too close together for you to adequately respond to and grade? It happens to the best of us. Mapping assignments can go a long way to helping ease these crunch times. For example, if you include a notation system about how much time you need to respond to and grade each assignment, you could spread them out with intention toward building time for you to more thoughtfully work through the submissions. Another consideration in your grading and feedback process is to think about the volume of direct instructor support you feel you have to provide versus facilitating rounds of peer feedback. A well-designed, accessible course that is thoughtfully mapped allows you to build in more supports and scaffolding, which sometimes relieves you from the necessity of feedback on every assignment item. Course mapping, then, becomes a wonderful opportunity for you to reconsider how you spend your time preparing for, then executing, the course design.

Finally, think about the workload for your students. More is not necessarily better in supporting students as they work toward particular outcomes in your course. Course mapping can also help you see how much time students may need to spend on assignments, which in terms of accessibility is a must for transparency's sake. Students need to know an estimated time for assignments or practice activities in the class. This helps them have more autonomy in how they plan their time in relation to any number of other responsibilities they may have (e.g. job, family, health concerns, activist groups, etc.). When developing your course map, do your best to estimate times for all activities that you plan in addition to building in a workable schedule for feedback turnarounds. Know that you may miss the mark on some of these estimates, but this is where getting student feedback and reflecting/implementing changes become much more important.

Cohesion and alignment refer to connections between activities, assignments, and assessments and how these three components work toward learning outcomes and/or objectives. What's interesting about this topic is that we tend to view cohesion and alignment as important for instructors, but we too often underestimate the benefits of revealing alignment to students. In terms of accessibility, clear alignment between assignments and assessments helps students understand the relevance of their work, and when they have clarity as to how an activity connects to their learning goals, students increase their engagement and learn more overall. Relevance of their work is imperative for many students to really connect with the work of a course. When students don't understand the exigence of an assignment beyond fulfilling a specific, course-restrictive goal, engagement can certainly become an issue. From an instructor perspective, if you struggle to articulate relevance and the ability to transfer the skills of an assignment outside of your course, this may be a time for you to reconsider the way the content is being taught and measured in your course. But, perhaps most importantly: a clear relationship between assessments and assignments offers students methods for how to understand your expectations. Some students can simply follow the guidelines, look at an example, and then intuit what you need them to do. Others desire to understand the value judgments you will be making on their work so they know how to best spend their time. The key here is to offer options that are equitable in use whether students choose to rely mostly on the guidelines, assessment criteria, or both.

Methods and Application

Approaches to course mapping vary from instructor to instructor, and much like learning and processing, mapping techniques come in a variety of shapes and sizes. A course map offers a big picture view of the course, so while the amount of detail will vary, there are four overarching layers to consider:

- Learning objectives/outcomes at both the course and module levels
- Assessments/major assignments
- Scaffolding toward major assignments
- Mapping out content

The layers of your course map will depend on your goals, and multiple techniques of mapping can be combined in different ways. Mapping is time consuming – there's no doubt about it. And at times, it can be quite daunting. Should you feel overwhelmed mapping your course, this is where collaborating with a colleague becomes so helpful. For example, Cat and Ashlyn both work in the same department, share many of the same conceptual frameworks for teaching and research, but both map courses very differently. Cat chooses to build a scaffolded table map with dates and shorthand notes, while Ashlyn chooses to build out assignments in an LMS working backwards from major assignments. Both have their advantages, but what works best is actually the two of them working together in their respective strength areas. Cat plots out a schedule of the weeks with major deadlines and basic scaffolding, while Ashlyn builds course assignments and navigation design in the LMS, ultimately benefiting both instructors and more importantly – students.

If you've struggled with the notion of modules before, you're not alone. Our best advice is to avoid overthinking how to break up your course. If you've already done the work of mapping your major assignments, you likely see natural units or modules emerging. In the event you are still uncertain as to the major assignments for your course (especially if this is a new prep where you have been given carte blanche to build) start by asking yourself: what do students need to know by the time they leave this course? Another equally important question to consider: what do the institution, department, or colleagues believe is important to convey in this course? Sometimes starting with these two questions is a great place for you to begin to envision what the major assignments are that would help students demonstrate their knowledge or application of course objectives. From here, you might consider how you would assess these assignments, then work reflexively. Think about: what do you need to assess? How is this assessment contradicting or supporting what I am asking students to actually do? And then of course, work in reverse: what is the best way to measure the students mastery of certain objectives? Is there room for creativity or perhaps a unique combination of objectives that would allow more content to be assessed in one place, thus ultimately helping with workload?

For our purposes, we will discuss mapping each layer separately (e.g., learning objectives, course level vs. module objectives, major assignments, content, and modules) and then offer alternatives for combining elements in the Models in Practice section of this chapter.

Mapping Learning Objectives

Learning objectives offer insights into the learning that takes place in your course, for both you and your students. Simply put, learning objectives state what students will be able to do by the end of a learning sequence, activity, unit, module, and/or course. Note that objectives should be written for student understanding, which means a good bit of translation is necessary on your part. For this reason, writing learning objectives can be difficult. For our purposes here, however, the goal is to map the learning across the course, so we will simplify this concept. If you feel this is something you want to explore further, we have a list of recommended resources at the end of this chapter.

The key to writing learning objectives is to remember that they should be measurable and specific, which means you should be able to see and measure the specific skill or concept in a student's submission. Our first piece of advice is to try to avoid getting hung up on the notion of measuring your students' work. There are many forms of measurement, only one of which is a grade in the form of numbers or letters, but there are others that you likely employ already in your feedback to students. Think of "measurable" as a way to let your students know how close or far away they are from applying a concept or performing a skill.

For Students: Learning objectives provide students with clarity as to

- What they will be expected to do
- What they will be assessed on
- What they will be able to do upon completion of the module/unit/course

For Instructors: The act of writing learning objectives provides faculty clarity as to

- What details should be included on an assignment description
- What learning sequences are needed to support student success
- What/how to assess student submissions

One word of caution is to avoid writing objectives as assessments, meaning that a strong objective focuses on skills rather than the assignment. The best way to avoid this pitfall is to keep asking yourself what students will be able to do with the skill they are working toward. For example, if you ask students to create a slideshow that shares their research findings, the objective isn't the ability to "create a slideshow" or "share research findings." You must ask yourself what students will be able to do after completing the slideshow. What will they be able to do after sharing their research findings? The objective will likely vary according to your course goals, but perhaps one of the following objectives might capture it:

- By the end of this assignment, students should be able to apply Universal Design principles using a digital design platform.
- By the end of this course, students should be able to synthesize ideas across multiple secondary sources.

Another way to conceive of strong learning objectives is to consider what you want students to be able to take from your class and apply it elsewhere. This can certainly fall within the scope of other academics, or what we would encourage more strongly is that you are inviting students to hone skills that can be applied to many different spaces, be they academic, personal, professional, or civic. From the student perspective, having a concrete set of objectives that can extend beyond the classroom helps them to develop marketable skills as well as a way to think about learning as an iterative process that extends far beyond the sphere of school.

Course-Level vs. Module-Level Objectives

Sometimes course-level objectives are mandated from your department or institution, but if you are tasked with writing your own, then we have a few tips and tricks to help you. First, aim for four to six objectives. Second, consider the big picture of your course and your goals: What are the most important concepts, ideas, or skills that you want students to learn? Keep in mind that course-level objectives are broad skills that should be measurable.

Module objectives (or unit or section objectives) are the smaller skills that students develop while working toward course-level objectives. We will use module, unit, and section interchangeably throughout the text and specifically in this chapter. First, think of the word "module" as a general term for chunks of learning in your course. We'll talk about ways of chunking course content later, but in general, you want to consider one module, unit, or assignment at a time, and think about what concepts, ideas, or skills you want students to learn. What do students need to be able to do to complete a given module, unit, or assignment? And these narrower skills should help students build up to the broader skills articulated in your course level objectives. These connections between module objectives and course objectives are referred to as alignment.

The act of mapping objectives allows you to work toward alignment between the content of the course (what you're teaching) and the assessments (what makes up the course grade). This is another area that's often overlooked or neglected during the course design process. We've found that creating an alignment map of objectives holds instructors accountable to students' learning. To understand how this neglect occurs, it might help to think about the enormous gap in knowledge between instructors and students. The instructor understands the larger learning goals through their expert lens, but students must rely on assignment descriptions and grading rubrics to determine what the instructor values or expects within a given assignment. We'll talk more about writing accessible assignments in the chapters on "Assignments" and "Content Development," but for now, consider the work of writing and aligning learning objectives as one step toward translating and revealing assessment expectations to your students.

Mapping Major Assignments

This technique works great for balancing workload for both you and your students, and it's fairly simple. Start with a calendar view of your semester, and then plot the major assignments across the semester as you see fit. Think of this map as an alternative to the semester calendar you might provide on a syllabus. Mapping out major assignments also offers you an opportunity to separate the course into discrete units or modules that build toward a larger end product of some sort. Thus, plotting core projects is an integral step in developing a course flow that can have a positive cascading effect on the scaffolding and support you build in for students. Keep in mind that when you start building out lessons and activities that support your major assignments, you may find that you need more or less time on a particular assignment. As we've already mentioned, mapping is an iterative and fluid process.

We've found that a map of major assignments becomes a resource to track where you are in the course, and to make notes of issues that arise so you can make revisions later. This map view also helps you budget your feedback and grading time across each week. For example, if you know that an assignment in Week 3 of the course will take more time to read and respond to, you can intentionally plan ungraded practice activities to grant you space and time for in-depth feedback. This ensures that you aren't overwhelmed and that your students feel supported and guided. This layer of a course map functions as a tool for both planning and time management.

Mapping Out the Content

Scaffolding refers to the learning sequence a student takes through a major assignment or concept. This often-neglected step in course design might be the most important. How does a student build a base of knowledge toward demonstrating or enacting a skill? What activities and experiences best support them toward assessing their understanding? Similar to a calendar or schedule provided on your syllabus, a scaffolding plan provides an overview of activities and assignments for the whole course. Some instructors start their planning process from such a map. A scaffolding plan includes resources, activities, lessons, assignments, and assessments. Think of it as a tool to help you visualize what students are learning, how they are learning, and how you know they are learning. Done correctly, it reveals any gaps or disconnects that might exist in your course or any of its assignments.

The big question when laying out scaffolding is: what do students need to know or practice to get from where they are currently to where they need to be for assessment? Specifically, you should consider what concepts you should teach and in what order. For example, if you have an assignment that asks students to conduct research and create a slideshow that shares their findings, there are multiple concepts they need to understand and have practiced to be successful. Some of what you decide to teach will depend on the course level (freshman vs. upper level), while other decisions will depend on the larger focus of the course (developing writing skill vs. mastering disciplinary content). We go into even more depth about this in the chapter on Scaffolding.

Mapping Course Modules

Yet another layer of mapping involves how to present content to your students. Some instructors find it helpful to present the course based on weekly activities and assignments, while others visualize the course around major assignments or units (Figures 7.1, 7.2). There is no right or wrong way to lay out your course. We encourage you to do what makes the most sense for you and your goals.

As instructors all experienced in writing studies, you might think we all map the same way, when in fact, this is far from true.

Models in Practice (Figures 7.1–7.2)

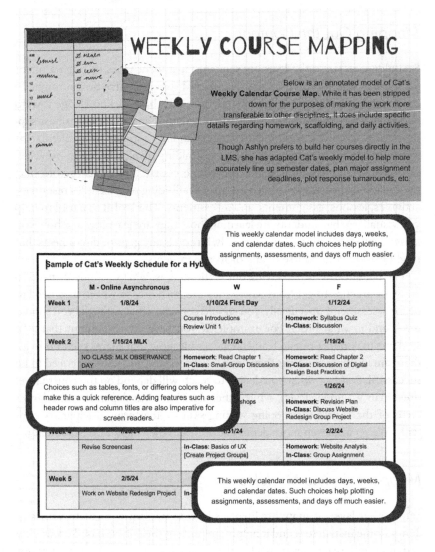

Figure 7.1 An annotated example of Cat's weekly course map design. Key features of this model are the use of weeks, dates, tables, color, and font emphasis

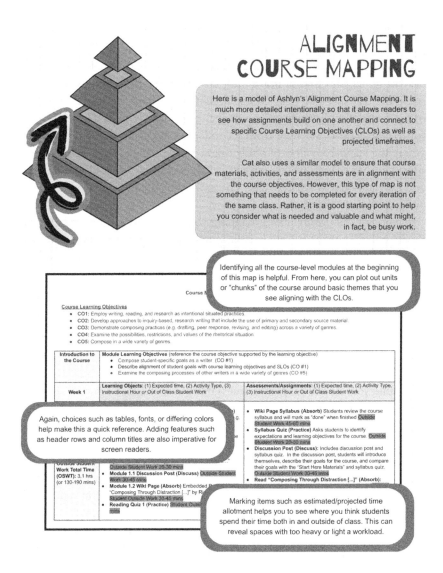

Figure 7.2 An annotated example of Ashlyn's course alignment mapping. Key features of this design include estimated time for assignments and course alignment notations

Putting Your Layers Together

As we've mentioned previously, course maps come in different forms, depending on needs and goals. The good news is that you can choose to keep your map layers separate, or you can put them together into one larger map. The key here is to be willing to try something a little different and perhaps time-consuming from the outset to make better use of your own time while ultimately better supporting students. Lists, visual maps, hand-drawn, typed, short-hand notes – all are fair game in helping you understand the trajectory of your course design even if you are limited in terms of course content flexibility. Even shell courses that are passed from instructor to instructor can benefit from secondary mapping as it may reveal areas where the standard course of study might be lacking. In short, mapping is a must because it helps us take inventory of our timing, scaffolding, support, and expectations, which inevitably change as our student needs, preferences, and populations change.

If you are still unsure about mapping your own course from scratch, you might consider mapping out a colleague's course from whatever platform or structure they use. Sometimes seeing the connections (or lack thereof) in other courses becomes a revealing exercise in what we need to do to best prepare our students. Don't be afraid – take the leap. And though at times you may stumble – or even just flat crash and burn – the iterative mapping process is still worth it.

Checklist

- [ ] Build your course map with accessibility in mind, for both your own use and as a tool for identifying barriers of access for your students.
- [ ] What gaps in your course design process can mapping potentially help you solve? Understanding what you want to get from a course map will help determine what layout/platform would work best for you.
- [ ] Once you figure out what mapping strategy works best for you, consider creating a ready-to-go template that can save you time each semester.
- [ ] Get in the habit of revisiting your course map regularly, including after each semester ends, so you can identify and highlight activities/timelines that could be improved.
- [ ] Consider talking through the pacing, scaffolding, and support offered in your course at the end of each semester with students offering them an informal opportunity to give feedback on what worked/needs improvement. We discuss this method in the "Scaffolding" chapter.
- [ ] Remember that course maps can be as detailed or as sparse as you see fit. What your course map looks like and contains is determined by you and your needs.

Further Reading and Resources

Course Mapping

Hartley, B., & Cha, A. (n.d.). The online course mapping guide. *Coursemapguide.com*. https://www.coursemapguide.com/

Jensen, J. L., Bailey, E. G., Kummer, T. A., & Weber, K. S. (2017). Using backward design in education research: A research methods essay. *Journal of Microbiology & Biology Education*, *18*(3), 18.3.50. https://doi.org/10.1128/jmbe.v18i3.1367

Rhoads, S., & Rocha-Hidalgo, J. (2020, November 30). *Designing a course and syllabus in psychological science*. https://www.apa.org/science/leadership/students/course-syllabus

Seok Nam, S. (2020). Integrating backward design principles for course curriculum planning. *Enhancing Pedagogy* Q2S. https://scholarworks.lib.csusb.edu/q2sep/219

Stearns Center for Teaching and Learning – George Mason University. (2023, November 29). Course Mapping. https://stearnscenter.gmu.edu/knowledge-center/course-and-curriculum-redesign/course-mapping/

Wiggins, G. P., & McTighe, J. (2005). *Understanding by design* (Expanded 2nd ed.). Association for Supervision and Curriculum Development.

Writing Learning Objectives

Alonso, F., López, G., Manrique, D., & Viñes, J. M. (2008). Learning objects, learning objectives and learning design. *Innovations in Education and Teaching International*, *45*(4), 389–400. https://doi.org/10.1080/14703290802377265

Chatterjee, D., & Corral, J. (2017). How to write well-defined learning objectives. *The Journal of Education in Perioperative Medicine*, *19*(4), 1–E610. https://doi.org/10.46374/volxix-issue4-chatterjee

Schneider, M. C., & Johnson, R. L. (2018). *Using formative assessment to support student Learning objectives* (1st ed.). London: Routledge.

Scaffolding

8

Introduction/Overview

As we've mentioned before, some instructors start designing their course by building the site first, and then they go back and do some of the mapping techniques described in our chapter on Course Mapping. Again, there is no right or wrong way to do this work. For teacher-designers, the thought of a course map is daunting. Instead, some folks may choose to work backwards from major assignments to identify smaller steps, then create a skeletal outline of the course. In fact, the work of course design might mean that you move back and forth between the course site and your mapping documents, so for you, thinking about your class in terms of scaffolding may be helpful as a first step – or perhaps a tenth step in your process. This chapter offers strategies for the work of fleshing out assignment steps and the sequencing of larger assignment movements, aka, scaffolding.

What Is Scaffolding?

Scaffolding is our way of developing the pathway from introducing a concept or assignment all the way through to when a student can demonstrate understanding through an assessment activity or submission (Bean, 2001; Shepard, 2005; MacLeod & van der Veen, 2020; Kalra, n.d.). Scaffolding includes resources, activities, lessons, assignments, and assessments. Think of it as a tool to help you visualize what students are learning, how they are learning, and how you know they are learning (Parks, 2022). Another way to think about scaffolding is the notion of taking students through intentional steps as they build toward larger assignments (Saulnier et al., 2021), like the development of a final portfolio that curates artifacts of learning.

DOI: 10.4324/9781003485476-9

Let's consider the example of a portfolio in more depth. Portfolios are used across different disciplines for many different purposes, but the unifying element is that they are meant to show development of skills over time along with relevant annotations about the work presented (Scott, 2010; Farrell & Seery, 2019; Janssens et al., 2022). Lengths and types of artifacts can certainly vary, but demonstrating a level of mastery of carefully selected materials is key. Now, even this two-sentence general description implies a lot of scaffolding work necessary to help students successfully complete this assignment. Lower stakes activities would need to be designed to help students be selective about their examples; models would have to be available, especially for visual or tactile learners; and clear expectations must be outlined in terms of what is being assessed and why. It's possible to address all these elements in a complex set of assignment guidelines, but the fact that portfolios are also contextual (e.g., an art portfolio is going to look different than an engineering portfolio), what it means to provide an example, how to curate, and the type/level of assessments are specific enough to a discipline or course to warrant thorough scaffolding toward the final product. Add to this equation the varied needs and preferences of students, and faculty can very quickly become overwhelmed with how to imagine a pathway to the end goal or major assignment.

While never easy, thoughtfully scaffolding a course is a must not only for student success but also for uncovering what truly matters in your class. Sometimes we get into ruts where we continue to do an assignment or activity that is ultimately dated because students are at a different place in their learning abilities or technology acumen. Scaffolding thus becomes an exercise in slowing down the course development process to the level at which one can decide what is truly important, what is practically needed to support learning, what is sentimental, and what is detrimental since it no longer serves a viable function. It can be painful. It can be infuriating. It can be challenging. But, more importantly, the systematic scaffolding of a course can be liberating in that it assists instructors in being more judicious and mindful of their own time as well as students', while also revealing areas for improvement or stability in the overall course design.

Scaffolding and Accessibility

Scaffolding is yet another tool for complicating our understanding and approach to accessibility by drawing our focus toward the pathway through an assignment. This requires keen attention to the finer details of a course, particularly when considering how to make the course road map accessible to a variety of students. For every student to have a means to success, gaps and barriers must be identified and then removed. Yet again, another issue of instructor time commitment and labor rears its head here: identifying barriers and gaps is a time-consuming process that requires a teacher-designer to intuit a tolerance for error, have a working knowledge about the specific populations that make up their courses, and a good sense of what supports them must be internally or externally provided in the class. This is a tall order, and like the course mapping or objectives, it can be overwhelming.

That said, we like to think of this book, and indeed this chapter, as a *model* for scaffolding accessible course design principles in class development. For example, we started with a big overall picture in our chapter on Course Mapping, then moved through the specific elements (e.g. navigation, assignments, content, etc.). This book design, like your scaffolded assignments, means that you help students build skills working toward an assessment, generally less difficult to more difficult and low stakes to high stakes. Where our text as an example deviates from the course design you might do depends on what you find difficult or easy as a starting point in your planning process. Cat, for instance, finds course mapping as a logical and simple starting point, while Ashlyn prefers to start with assignment development. In this way, considering your pathway through course design, your own needs and preferences for what steps to take and when, might help you visualize scaffolding student pathways through your major assignments.

For example, in your course, you might set a more restrictive pathway for learning, like a pre-test to gauge the knowledge base of students for credit if they complete the test regardless of score. Then you might move to a practice activity that includes peer or instructor response. The design of these steps, or building blocks, that help students gauge their understanding and build skills as they progress toward an assessment are critical for accessibility. In addition to these pathfinding steps, multiple modalities of resources/ assignments (e.g. aural, visual, tactical) and access points (e.g., navigation) must be included, and scaffolding is a means to locate these more student-driven needs/preferences.

The main goal when considering accessibility and scaffolding is figuring out what each student needs in order to get from where they currently are to the point at which they are ready to be assessed. We have to also consider the fact that most students in our classes have varying degrees of knowledge on the content of the course, and with a course that an instructor has taught forward and backward for say ten years, it can become altogether too easy to fall into patterns of practice that aren't truly considering students first. To do this, we must consider *how to determine* what a student already knows, and more importantly, what gaps or barriers exist for their understanding of a concept. This is a recursive process that often has to be attempted with every iteration of the course (semester to semester, quarter to quarter, and even unit to unit within the same class). Too often, assumptions are made about what students bring to our courses, and these preconceived notions can lead to decisions that leave less prepared students lost, and high performing students frustrated. Even in courses with prerequisites, students will have varying levels of knowledge and depth of understanding from previous courses.

For example, in an advanced writing course with a prerequisite of first-year writing, some students will have performed well in their first-year writing course, while others will have barely scraped by. Their level of success or failure hinges on the overarching assumption that first-year writing courses teach students to compose generally for all college writing situations. Yet, first-year writing scholarship clearly delineates its work as the study of writing and composing practices, analyzing the rhetorical situation of a piece of communication and making choices to best fit said audience and genre. Now, these questions can certainly help a student know the kinds of questions to ask when looking for help on drafting a biology report, but the truth is the biology faculty member has to demonstrate how to do this type of writing as a biologist. Unless addressed with intention and within the lens of the specific discipline you are working in, the gaps in their readiness will cause those less prepared to ultimately fail. An accessible course design requires the identification and offsetting of these gaps and barriers so that all students, no matter their performance in previous courses, have a clear pathway to success.

This is a good time to point out practical limitations. No matter how hard you work on scaffolding, there will always be some students with learning gaps. You can only make choices that enhance accessibility. You can never guarantee that every student *will* succeed. On the positive side, identifying learning gaps while a course is in process is a great way to get real-time participatory feedback from your students. As the learners/users in your class, they can provide insight on other resources, models, or scaffolding that might be useful. And though you may not be able to implement said changes right away or even in the near future, it does give some space for thought about how to best carve out a clear road map to success.

Methods and Applications

Just like we've mentioned before, the work of scaffolding might occur at different points in your design process. Likewise, there are different approaches to building out pathways through an assignment. Some instructors design with a top-down approach, starting with course level goals and objectives and narrowing down toward the smaller elements of the course. Others prefer to start with smaller scale items like assignments and lessons, and then work their way out. Just like all other aspects of course design, there is no right or wrong approach. It is important that you learn more about what may work best for your way of planning and designing your course.

Guiding Questions When Scaffolding

- What is the learning goal?
- What do students already know and what have they already done prior to the introduction of this assignment or concept?
- What artifact/activity will students submit for assessment/feedback?
- What skills are students practicing and/or demonstrating progression in?
- How will you assess students' submissions?
- What new things will students need to know to be able to practice or perform the learning goal?
- What activities will best provide scaffolding for students?
- What resources are most appropriate and effective for the activities?

Notice that the preceding questions are in the form of a bulleted list and not numbered. We intentionally avoided the use of numbers so that it would not imply some type of linear order (e.g., you must identify the learning goal before formulating some type of activity or assessment). Our goal here is to show the flexible nature of course design work, and we encourage you to start with the easiest question in this list and work progressively toward areas that you may feel are more difficult to attain. We recommend this strategy because we often get bogged down in linear thinking in such a way that we are neither efficient nor productive in course planning, which inevitably impacts students and creates accessibility issues. Additionally, having what you would consider smaller successes with questions you find easiest to answer often generates new ideas and thinking that can help you address the more complicated aspects of scaffolding. Now let's take time to work through these questions offering some examples on how one might approach addressing each item.

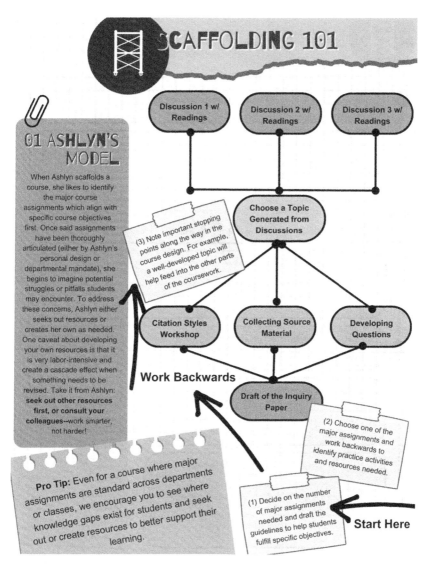

Figure 8.1 Ashlyn's method for scaffolding in a course. Her approach involves beginning with major assignments and gradually working backward to practice activities and resources

Model in Practice

In the spirit of the type of accessibility we espouse throughout the manual, we recognize some readers may wish to have a definition of scaffolding,

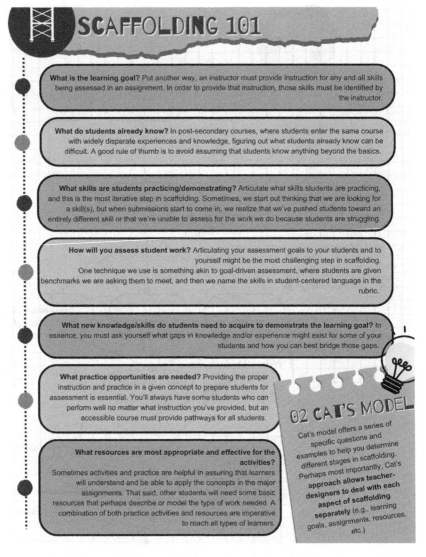

Figure 8.2 Cat's method for scaffolding. This approach offers a series of questions starting with the overall learning goal and gradually working toward recognition of existing student skills, assessments, resources, and supports

followed by written examples, and then a short review of the literature that grounds these practices, but for others, a visual is needed. Conceptually speaking, describing scaffolding beyond a definition and series of examples is particularly difficult for one of our authors – Ashlyn. For her, course scaffolding must take shape in naming, identifying, and structuring a visual that follows a sequence to an end goal; in short, Ashlyn has to see a physical pathway to completion / assessment. Here we have offered an annotated visual for scaffolding one learning sequence in a writing course. We start by identifying a concept or learning objective and then scaffold toward the culminating artifact that assesses students' learning.

Putting Your Scaffolding Layers Together

As we have demonstrated throughout this chapter, there are many ways to approach scaffolding – starting from learning objectives and working backwards to sequencing, starting with small activities to build to larger assignments, and vice versa. If we could underscore one piece of solid advice more than others: start by identifying large- and small-scale assignments, then ask yourself what students need to accomplish these tasks, what's worked in the past, and where were previous gaps in learning knowledge. Such questions will help you become better equipped to tailor learning sequences in pathways that make sense for your specific discipline and course. Even courses which have shells or prescriptive content can benefit from outlining the scaffolding from one assignment to the next. Doing so can often reveal unintentional assessments that do not, in fact, appropriately prepare students to tackle.

If you are still unsure how scaffolding might take shape in your classroom, we again encourage you to collaborate with a colleague or colleagues. Take an opportunity to talk through what students do in your class, how they are supported, and what you value most in your assessment. From here, you could invite your colleague to see if your short description matches what is designed in your actual course. Granted, this level of collaboration with a colleague can be intimidating, especially when we work so hard to develop quality courses, but having another pair of eyes cannot be understated. As writing studies and design professionals, we recognize that collaboration is an iterative process, but this can be quite challenging if and when intellectual property is at stake or guidelines for your course are quite stringent at the department or institution level. But, engaging in this activity at any small level of collaboration does open a world of possibilities.

Checklist

☐ Build the sequencing of your course with accessibility in mind, for both your own use and as a tool for identifying barriers of access for your students.

☐ Identify potential barriers or gaps in student knowledge based on what you know of your student population, support services available at your institution, and the time/labor you have to devote to the issues that arise.

☐ Start with the assignments that seem the easiest for you to scaffold. What assignments have been particularly successful in the past? Identify what and why they were successful. How then could you leverage some of these strategies in less successful assignments?

☐ Consider assignments that have been challenging to scaffold in the past. Where are the learning gaps among students? Consider inviting student feedback on what they need to help them feel more supported/successful with your sequence design.

☐ Use the following questions to flesh out the pathways in your class:

  (1) What is the learning goal?

  (2) What do students already know and what have they already done prior to the introduction of this assignment or concept?

  (3) What artifact/activity will students submit for assessment/feedback?

  (4) What skills are students practicing and/or demonstrating progression in?

  (5) How will you assess students' submissions?

  (6) What new things will students need to know to be able to practice or perform the learning goal?

  (7) What activities will best provide scaffolding for students?

  (8) What resources are most appropriate and effective for the activities?

☐ Identify priorities for scaffolding in terms of lower order and higher-level learning objectives. Assignments that are assessed on a much larger scale may be the best place to spend your time before addressing more lower-stakes assessments.

References and Resources

Bean, J.C. (2001). *Engaging ideas: The professor's guide to integrating writing, critical thinking, and active learning in the classroom*. San Francisco, CA: Jossey-Bass.

Farrell, O., & Seery, A. (2019). "I am not simply learning and regurgitating information, I am also learning about myself": Learning portfolio practice and online distance students. *Distance Education, 40*(1), 76–97. https://doi.org/10.1080/01587919.2018.1553565

Janssens, O., Haerens, L., Valcke, M., Beeckman, D., Pype, P., & Embo, M. (2022). The role of ePortfolios in supporting learning in eight healthcare disciplines: A scoping review. *Nurse Education in Practice, 63*, 103418–103418. https://doi.org/10.1016/j.nepr. 2022.103418

Kalra, J. (n.d.). Scaffolded assessments. *Encouraging Academic Integrity Through Intentional Assessment Design.* https://pressbooks.bccampus.ca/encourageacademicintegrity/front-matter/acknowledgments/

MacLeod, M., & van der Veen, J. T. (2020). Scaffolding interdisciplinary project-based learning: a case study. *European Journal of Engineering Education, 45*(3), 363–377. https://doi.org/10.1080/03043797.2019.1646210

Park, S. (2022). A study on visual scaffolding design principles in web-based learning environments. *Electronic Journal of E-Learning, 20*(2), 180–200. https://doi.org/10.34190/ejel. 20.2.2604

Saulnier, J., Johnson, C. M., & Whalen, K. (2021). Scaffolded research assignment analysis for a required first year course. *The Journal of Academic Librarianship, 47*(1), 102293. https://doi.org/10.1016/j.acalib.2020.102293

Scott, S. G. (2010). Enhancing reflection skills through learning portfolios: An empirical test. *Journal of Management Education, 34*(3), 430–457. https://doi.org/10.1177/105256 2909351144

Shepard, L. A. (2005). Linking formative assessment to scaffolding. In *Educational Leadership* (Vol. 63, Issue 3, pp. 66). Association for Supervision and Curriculum Development.

Navigation

9

Introduction/Overview

Most instructors house their courses on a site of some sort like a learning management system (e.g., Canvas, Blackboard, Moodle, or another iteration of LMS that has yet to be developed). Some institutions require instructors to use predesigned course templates while others offer little to no guidance in this area. Some institutions have instructional designers housed in a separate unit who serve a wide variety of faculty and levels of subject-area expertise. The level of services that instructional designers provide differs for individual courses or instructors; some complete all course design work, others work more as facilitators or guides, stepping in when instructor-design expertise is limited or still developing. No matter what platform you use or how much design work you're expected to do, this chapter offers insights to help you link course content and assignments in clear and accessible pathways. Even when courses are fairly set in terms of a design/shell/pathway, there is often still wiggle room to create additional layers of navigation in a way that will best serve students while still not violating the expectations of template use.

What Is Navigation?

For our purposes, navigation refers to the linked pathway through your course site, the intentional structure you create so that students can find their way through your activities, lessons, and assignments. This includes built-in navigation features like top-level menu links and instructor-designed areas like landing page layout and hyperlinks within and across course pages. Now, while it may be tempting to rely on a platform's built-in navigational features, and while this works for some users, it doesn't necessarily work for

DOI: 10.4324/9781003485476-10

everyone. Consider the fact that many technology tools are often user-tested at the end stage of development where large-scale changes would be costly (Nielsen, 2006; Oswal, 2014; Lavin et al., 2022). This fact alone implies that testing by users may reveal some pretty serious navigational problems that require some type of system overhaul, which is not ideal. The platform itself may work for the "generalizable user," but let's be honest – the students in our courses are rarely so neatly confined to such boxes. And if students don't conform to categories of users with a set of specific needs that are internal to the LMS, then navigational redundancies must be built or facilitated by the instructor (Mahaffey & Walden, 2019; Walden, 2022).

Let's take our teacher hat off for just a moment and consider navigation through the lens of a ship's captain. And by the way this is dealer's choice: you can take to sea like Captain Jack Sparrow or boldly go into space like Captain Janeway – either void will do in this metaphor. When you hear the word *navigation*, you might visualize a ship sailing across the ocean or traveling through space, as the captain relies on both instinct and knowledge to steer the ship from one port to another. Any captain worth their salt understands that relying on only one navigation tool could prove fatal. Any number of obstacles might arise. Technology might fail. Hurricanes and ion storms might limit visibility. For this reason, redundant navigation tools are used to set bearings while at sea or in space, including compasses, radar, sonar, star charts, long-range sensors, and landmarks, and some tools are appropriate for one expedition whereas another might be best for a different adventure (think tricoders). Our point is that even if all these tools aren't used by every captain on every sailing trip, they are available for use.

Navigation and Accessibility: Now, Where Was That Assignment?

In terms of accessibility, navigation is critical for multiple reasons. For starters, if the navigation within your course is confusing or unintuitive, students may struggle to find what they need in terms of learning materials, assignments, or resources. This can create a sense of frustration and wasted time, hindering students' ability to complete coursework. Consider also that if students cannot locate lessons and resources necessary to master concepts, their overall engagement with course content will be limited to surface level understanding since they will need to expend some of their limited cognitive energy on searching rather than focusing on course content. As faculty, we can sometimes wrongly assume that a student is unengaged with the course when, in fact, their cognitive load is being heavily focused on figuring out how to move through the layout of the course. We may find ourselves being more frustrated still when questions during class sessions or individual meetings perpetually revolve around locating course material. That moment where we think "Good grief, it's in the resources section of our class, and I've said that seventeen times," our students are thinking "Where the hell is this assignment?" The solution to both these frustrations is again, navigational redundancies.

This of course sounds great in theory, particularly when instructors retain primary (or perhaps sole) control of their course content and design development. For those that use templated courses with strict adherence expectations, diverse navigational pathways seem like a mirage. Think about an entry level engineering course which reviews some of the fundamental tenets of engineering. Specific modules/units are laid out in a progressive sequence with short knowledge-check quizzes, followed by a basic lab that applies the concepts measured in the quizzes, and then a final unit test. Units in this course follow this model throughout each of the modules, with the course culminating in some type of capstone project where students write an extended paper that discusses the major concepts of the course and how they see this applying to the work as an engineer in the field. These assignments and activities are nonnegotiable no matter who is teaching the course, and so is the basic navigational setup of the course shell. The operative word here is *shell*, implying that there is wiggle room in terms of other support assignments and navigational features that you could build into the course. Shells in course design are only meant as a starting point in terms of navigation; it is the most basic form of how to move through a class, but it doesn't necessarily account for all the various learning needs and preferences students may have.

Let's say this Engineering 101 course template has all of the assignments/activities/resources laid out on a homepage according to due dates and are divided into larger concept chunks aka units. You have been instructed to keep all the same due dates, material, and unit markers, but what if you sequenced the course material further in terms of weeks? Or could you perhaps consider developing weekly overview pages that chart explicitly the course work and homework assignments? Would a homepage be useful that links to the larger course units? Is there space in the course structure to add additional low-stakes practice assignments? Notice that none of these questions are technically in violation of the standardized template, but what they do offer are more navigational pathways that can improve student engagement in the course. Multiple points of access is a fundamental grounding principle to any well-developed class, as students – and faculty for that matter – have differing ways of staying on track in a course.

Even between us as the authors, the way we move through a course is very different. Cat prefers to proceed through a course by going through a list of assignments split into weeks. Ashlyn needs a weekly calendar page that functions like a checklist. All are valid ways of moving through the class, but the key here is to have these variations available in the navigation so that students can feel supported, successful, and grounded. Granted, planning this level of navigational diversity can be intimidating and time consuming, yet this labor has a huge payoff in terms of student satisfaction. From a purely selfish instructor perspective, students are less apt to feel lost and overwhelmed, while also being willing to try things out themselves instead of always immediately running to you as the teacher.

On the other end of the spectrum, you may have the freedom to develop a course carte blanche, which can be both invigorating and challenging at the same time. When presented with this option, the key is to try not to do everything, everywhere, all at once. Our recommendation would be to perhaps start with the "Course Mapping" chapter to identify your major assignments and then move to the "Scaffolding" chapter to see what smaller sequences might be needed in the course. Doing so will help you to chart a more linear trajectory, after which you can start to identify other ways of chunking the material. Think of it this way: besides a linear progression, what additional pathways may be helpful to your students? A weekly module perhaps? Clusters of larger concepts? A calendar? A landing page that navigates to the most current unit or week? An automatically generated to-do list? Perhaps there should be a place where students can view all the assignments divided by grading categories? The point is to start with the sequencing through a course that makes the most sense to you, then think about other ways students may need to engage with the material. Collaborating with seasoned colleagues is another fantastic way to intuit potential problems, build in a navigational tolerance for error, and generate redundant pathways through the class. And finally, when the course is near completion, enlisting student input on how well course navigation worked will give you clear insights on how to revise and prepare for the future.

Thus far, it may seem this chapter takes a somewhat dismal view of templated courses, when in fact, this is not the case. Templates or course shells are immensely helpful to those that haven't taught a course before, are new to the profession, or are one of many contingent faculty that spread their working load across multiple institutions with varying degrees of expectations. And even for those that may have the opportunity, time, and desire to devote to a wholly original course design, shells are a great place to start in terms of a manageable course load for students and faculty.

Methods and Applications

If you've mapped out your course, you might see a logical navigation system emerging. Perhaps you see modules as a good way to chunk content, or maybe it makes more sense to have students access coursework structured around weeks or even days. No matter what you're leaning toward, we encourage you to step back and consider some key guidelines before you set up your course navigation. To say that navigation is critical would be an understatement. To say that navigation is intuitive would be a misstatement. Accessible navigation is only achieved by both working within and sometimes against the limitations of a digital platform, and such actions are only possible through careful planning, consideration, and execution.

Guiding Questions for Building Navigation and Redundancies

Put another way, let's think about navigation in terms of levels: primary, secondary, and tertiary.

Primary Navigation

Primary navigation systems function as the backbone of your course, the central hub from which the rest of your course expands outward. Some LMS platforms are more templated than others, but most of them allow instructors to pick and choose which primary links they prefer for their landing page. Common primary navigation links to consider include the syllabus, major assignment descriptions, weekly overview pages, technical and academic support services, and other general course resources.

To best identify primary navigational features, consider:

- How do you want students to move through your course site? Units? Weeks? Days?
- What will your landing page look like or consist of?
- Is it necessary to let the LMS determine the landing page, or would instructor intervention be more appropriate here?
- What permanent, primary links are necessary?
- What opportunities for redundancies are needed with regards to the primary navigation system?

Secondary Navigation

Secondary navigation serves as the first layer of links outward from your hub; put another way – it serves as the second step away from the primary navigation. Think of this as the first level of dividing your course into chunks. Some instructors present content in weekly formats, while others want students to move through assignments in themes or units. Again, there's no right or wrong way to do this, but it is important to be consistent and logical. If you start out using themed modules, stick with it.

To best identify secondary navigational features, consider:

- What are the large-scale themes or concepts in this course that could be divided into modules or units?
- What are some short names for identified units or modules that accurately communicate the content therein?
- How often are you assigning coursework?
  - If you are finding a pattern of multiple times in a single week, then perhaps weeks may be a further division warranted at the secondary level beyond units.
  - If you have single submissions per week, weekly divisions may still work, but it may be best to consider keeping the larger-scale units rather than separation by week.
- If you were a student in this course, what sort of chunking would work for you as a learner? Think very carefully about this question simply because how you would chunk a course as an instructor may look different if you were a student.

Tertiary Navigation

An often overlooked but critical aspect of navigation relates to the intra- and inter-navigational links that help students move backward and forward across and between assignments, lessons, and resources. We will refer to this as tertiary navigation. For example, let's say you have a major assignment that includes several scaffolded minor assignments that move students toward the final submission. To help students understand the purpose of each minor assignment and how it fits into the bigger picture of the larger assignment and the course, you should continually provide hyperlinks to the full description, and likewise include links from the major assignment page to all activities and lessons that inform their final submissions.

To best identify tertiary navigational features, consider:

- What are the large-scale assignments and accompanying scaffolding?
- Are there knowledge gaps that could be addressed by further scaffolding?
- What resources are needed to assist in the completion of large-scale assignments?
- Where are there opportunities to create continuity between course assignments?
- What assignments must be completed before others?

Using this series of questions will help you identify the elements needed across the three levels of navigation. While it could be argued that you could limit these questions or even one of the levels like tertiary navigation, we would discourage you from doing so. These questions help to build an intuitive navigational design that works for many different types of learners, while also accounting for a tolerance of error in a way that helps students to see the interconnectivity of course content.

Model in Practice

For this chapter, we've chosen to offer primary, secondary, and tertiary levels of navigation as models. Understand that depending on your LMS or other tech-mediated space that you may use, like web conferencing software or cloud computing spaces, you may or may not need to incorporate all the levels of navigation we propose here. Though we believe it is best practice to include all three navigation pathways for maximum accessibility, limitations of the technology systems you are using, system administrative restrictions, departmental or university regulations, or even your own comfort level with the platform will dictate where you will spend your time. Simply starting with primary navigation, for example, can fundamentally change how students feel supported in your course, so if you have to make judicious choices about where to spend your time, we recommend that you develop a well-developed landing page that will help students move more seamlessly through the class content.

   NOTE: We deliberately did not incorporate any of our own screenshots from the LMS that we currently use as instructors. Instead, we offer illustrative models which highlight certain aspects of navigation that can be applied across platforms, regardless of the operating system or requirements.

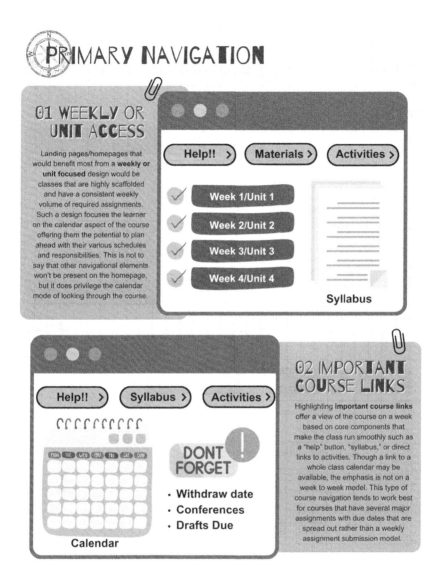

Figure 9.1 Illustration of how you can develop primary navigation features either by highlighting a weekly calendar view or major course links. Choosing the option that works best for you depends upon whether or not you have weekly course work or if the class follows a different work cycle

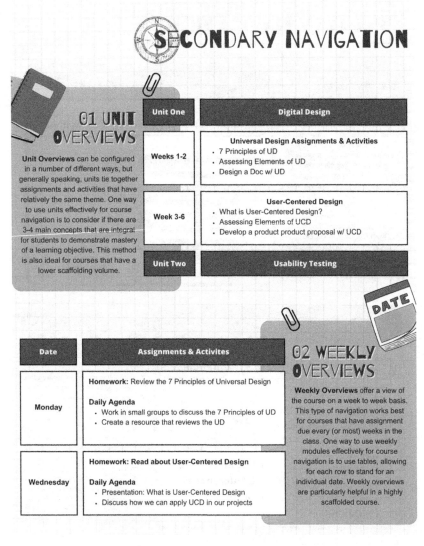

Figure 9.2 Demonstration of secondary navigation features such as dividing your course either into unit or weekly segments. To choose what works best, consider if your class has work due on a weekly basis or if there are larger assignments that require concept mastery. Larger assignments with spread-out due dates tend to work better for units, whereas weekly course work due dates work best for a week-by-week module

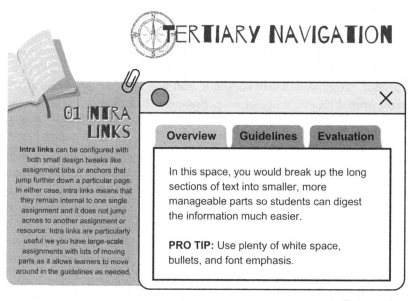

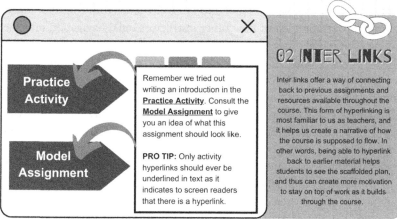

Figure 9.3 The difference between intra- and inter-hyperlinks built into course materials. Intra-links are helpful for written guidelines that are long and involved, thus using tabs or anchors is helpful to allow students to more freely move through the space

Putting Your Layers Together

As with our other chapters, navigation is a complex task that requires thoughtful consideration, application, and, at times, revision. And while learning management systems and institutional requirements can sometimes hinder/limit our navigational capabilities, our goal was to demonstrate how one might work through a range of restrictiveness or lack thereof. Even with the advent of built-in accessibility checkers, platforms still run the risk of unequal access for students with diverse learning needs, preferences, or cultural backgrounds. If we return to the sailing analogy, we can imagine that one captain might expect and be more experienced using a simple compass for navigation, while another might have only used digital tools like a GPS in their past. For both captains to succeed, the ship needs to have the full gamut of navigational tools available. Likewise, students come to our courses with very different backgrounds, experiences, and learning preferences. If we want them to have full access to all the learning resources we provide, we must offer multiple pathways through our course materials.

If you are still uncomfortable with what navigation can look like in your classroom platform, we encourage you to collaborate with colleagues. Just a simple conversation about how other instructors build navigation into their courses can reveal other methods for redundancies. Such course design work should never be done alone, and really the very fact that you are reading this book is a level of collaboration. For a few moments out of your day/week/month/year, you are thinking with us as writer-designers considering what affordances and constraints you have with course navigation. Though you may still feel your options may be limited either by technologies, institutional expectations, or even your personal technological skill sets, taking time to reflect on the possibilities of entry pathways is crucial. Such thinking helps you to identify potential opportunities for a more accessible course that is attentive to student needs and preferences, which ultimately embodies the spirit and practice of inclusive teaching/learning.

Checklist

- [ ] Consistency: Maintain consistency in navigation across the LMS. Users should be able to easily navigate between different sections, modules, or pages within the LMS without confusion. Consistently format and place hyperlinks, buttons, and navigation elements.
- [ ] Clear and Intuitive Labels: Use clear and intuitive labels that accurately describe the content or functionality to which you are linking.

☐ Logical Organization: Group related topics or modules together and provide clear pathways for learners to follow. Consider the learners' perspective and how they would naturally navigate through the course content. Well-structured navigation helps learners locate and access information efficiently.

References and Resources

Baldwin, S. J., & Ching, Y.-H. (2020). Guidelines for designing online courses for mobile devices. *TechTrends*, 64(3), 413–422. https://doi.org/10.1007/s11528-019-00463-6

Borgman, J. & McArdle, C. (2022). Continuous delivery: A PARS online course development cycle. *Computers and Composition*, 66, 1–16. https://doi.org/10.1016/j.compcom.2022.102741

Burgstahler, S. (2020). *Creating inclusive learning opportunities in higher education: A universal design toolkit* (pp. 47–48). Cambridge, MA: Harvard Education Press.

Conley, Q., Earnshaw, Y., & McWatters, G. (2020). Examining course layouts in blackboard: Using eye-tracking to evaluate usability in a learning management system. *International Journal of Human-Computer Interaction*, 36(4), 373–385. https://doi.org/10.1080/10447318.2019.1644841

Lavin, A., Gilligan-Lee, C. M., Visnjic, A., Ganju, S., Newman, D., Ganguly, S., Lange, D., Baydin, A. G., Sharma, A., Gibson, A., Zheng, S., Xing, E. P., Mattmann, C., Parr, J., & Gal, Y. (2022). Technology readiness levels for machine learning systems. *Nature Communications*, 13(1), 6039–6039. https://doi.org/10.1038/s41467-022-33128-9

Mahaffey, C. & Walden, A. (2019). # teachingbydesign: Complicating accessibility in the tech-mediated classroom. In K. Becnel (Ed.), *Emerging technologies in virtual learning environments* (pp. 38–66). Hershey, PA: IGI Global.

Muro, M. (n.d.). How to make your course navigation 10x better. *Proof Mango*. https://proofmango.com/make-online-course-navigation-better/

Nielsen, J. (2006). *User testing is not entertainment*. Nielsen Norman Group. Retrieved from https://www.nngroup.com/articles/user-testing-is-not-entertainment/

Oswal, S. (2014). Participatory design: barriers and possibilities. *Communication Design Quarterly Review*, 2(3), 14–19. https://doi.org/10.1145/2644448.2644452

Walden, A. C. (2022). Necessity is the mother of invention: Accessibility pre, inter, & post pandemic. *Computers and Composition*, 66, 102740. Accessed January 30, 2024. https://doi.org/10.1016/j.compcom.2022.102740

Index

Pages in *italics* refer to figures.

14994940R00077